Harvesting Spiritual Fruit

*Following God's Path to True Love,
Joy and Peace*

Jonathan Niemeyer

www.harvestingspiritualfruit.com

Harvesting Spiritual Fruit
by Jonathan Niemeyer

Printed in the United States of America

Library of Congress Control Number: 2002102676
ISBN 1-591600-22-7

Scripture taken from the HOLY BIBLE, NEW INTERNATIONAL VERSION®. NIV®. Copyright © 1973, 1978, 1984 by International Bible Society. Used by permission of Zondervan. All rights reserved.

Xulon Press
11350 Random Hills Road
Suite 800
Fairfax, VA 22030
(703) 279-6511
XulonPress.com

Dedication

To my unbelievable wife Jennifer and to our incredible little gifts from God—Alexandra and Benjamin

Acknowledgments

With appreciation to:

My Lord and Savior Jesus Christ who continues to amaze me with His infinite blessings.

My extended family and friends who tolerated my passion for writing and publishing this book.

My mother for always believing that I could rise above difficult circumstances and for loving me unconditionally.

My maternal grandparents for their extraordinary example of the ideal Christian marriage, and their steadfast commitment to truly live and breathe the fruit of the spirit.

My mother-in-law Gerri for her constant support of this effort and reading all twenty four drafts of this manuscript!

My father-in-law John for his encouragement and for proving that men really will read a good Christian Living book.

My son Benjamin, one of three reasons (the other two are below!) I can't wait to get out of the office every day.

My daughter Alexandra for first opening my eyes to the profound meaning of the fruit of the spirit.

And finally, my wife, Jennifer, the greatest of encouragers, for her love, friendship and unconditional support of me and of this labor of love.

Contents

Acknowledgments...vii

Introduction...xi

Chapter I   Fruit of the Spirit...................................17

Chapter II   Love..23

Chapter III   Joy..45

Chapter IV   Peace..53

Chapter V   Patience..57

Chapter VI   Kindness and Goodness.........................63

Chapter VII   Faithfulness..75

Chapter VIII   Gentleness..87

Chapter IX   Self-Control..101

Conclusion..107

Introduction

On September 11, 2001, all of America watched in horror as two hijacked commercial airliners were intentionally flown into the World Trade Center by malicious terrorists. Shortly thereafter, a third group of terrorists dive-bombed a passenger jet into the Pentagon, and a fourth group crashed an airliner just south of Pittsburgh, Pennsylvania, apparently thwarted by courageous passengers from its intended target—the White House or the United States Capitol. Thousands of innocent lives were extinguished in an instant, and thousands of others were burned or otherwise injured, their lives forever scarred, both physically and emotionally, by these acts of terror. Millions of Americans personally knew the victims or learned about their lives through the media's portrayal of the events of September 11th—the heartfelt pleas of loved ones holding up pictures of their missing sisters, brothers, moms, dads, and children, and tearful funerals and eulogies. By now in America, most of the tears have been wiped away, the fear has subsided, the unspeakable has now been spoken and accepted as fact, and our lives have continued. However, our American way of life seemed to be immeasurably changed that day. Anthrax deaths and hoaxes put a nation already on alert on pins and needles. The sound of a car backfiring or of a low-flying jet caused at least momentary fear. Normalcy in America was forever redefined.

A survey two months following September 11th revealed that ninety percent of people had experienced "emotional stress" due to the attacks. Over one-third of Americans donated blood or money or volunteered their time. Most importantly, ninety percent of Americans had turned to prayer or religion to cope with the attacks. A spiritual and patriotic renewal appeared to take hold in America. Was it superficial? Was it to be short lived? Or would the renewal be lasting, real, and tangible? Was it to be only a patriotic renewal, or would a true spiritual awakening follow? Only time will tell. Over time, it is possible that the good will, outpouring of financial and emotional support, increased church attendance, and patriotic fervor will recede. I hope not.

Unfortunately, although open displays of newfound patriotism remained high, the rush to prayer and to churches appeared to rapidly decline just months following the attacks. In a *New York Times* article dated November 26, 2001, entitled "As Attacks' Impact Recedes, A Return to Religion As Normal," Laurie Bernstein reported that, although Americans turned to religion in an outpouring that some religious leaders proclaimed was a spiritual "great awakening," most returned to their level of church attendance prior to the attacks. "I just don't see much indication that there has been a great awakening or a profound change in America's religious practices," said Frank M. Newport, editor-in-chief of the Gallup Poll. "It looks like people were treating this like a bereavement, a shorter-term funeral kind of thing, where they went to church or synagogue to grieve. But once past that, their normal churchgoing behavior passed back to where it was."

Ms. Bernstein also quoted Robert Wuthnow, director of the Center for the Study of Religion at Princeton University, in the article. He stated that the attacks did not upset

America's religious balance: one-quarter of the population devout, one-quarter secular, and one-half mildly interested. "We are in some ways a very religious country, especially compared to Western Europe," Mr. Wuthnow said. "But we're of two minds, and the other mind is that we really are pretty secular. *We are very much a country of consumers and shoppers, and we're quite materialistic.* And as long as we can kind of paste together a sense of control through our ordinary work and our ordinary purchases, we're pretty happy to do that" (italics added). Mr. Wuthnow's last comment is disheartening, but true. Modern America is first and foremost a materialistic society, and this "consumerism" is a religion unto itself. Breaking free from the iron grasp of such materialism, which runs contrary to Biblical principles and offers false hopes of "happiness," is a focus of this book.

Within a few days of September 11, 2001, my daughter, just a month into kindergarten at a Christian elementary school, was charged with reciting Galatians 5:22, 23, the "fruit of the spirit," from memory. In fact, although she was responsible for one short verse of scripture a month, the fruit of the spirit was the school's designated verse for the entire year. My daughter, my wife, and I practiced these two verses together for several days during September 2001. My wife and I listened intently to my daughter's sweet voice recite the fruit God wishes us to harvest and apply to our lives—love, joy, peace, patience, kindness, goodness, faithfulness, gentleness, and self-control. Just days later, I felt compelled to write the following letter to the editor of a local Cincinnati newspaper:

> After experiencing the varied emotions I am sure all have also felt over the past week—helplessness, fear, sadness, and anger—and having attended church numerous times this past week, seeking answers and praying for those who have lost their lives or family

members, one emotion is now overriding the others: hope. I am still deeply saddened, and still angry, but this past week has proven that America can once again regain its rightful position as a godly superpower, not just a military one.

Although I do not believe the events of September 11th occurred due to our country's moral decay over the past several decades, I do believe they offer the opportunity to get back to the basics upon which this country was founded. America has never been perfect. It has been scarred by slavery, racism, civil war, and crime, but America holds the most promise and hope of any civilization on earth.

With the assistance of the ACLU, the media, and the courts, God has been expunged from classrooms, our places of work, our televisions, our movies, and our "pop" culture. However, as the past week has taught us (and maybe taught our enemies), America has not forgotten its roots. Our Christian roots are still alive, but they need to be watered, fed, and nurtured back to full health.

How many times have you heard or read "God Bless America" this past week? It is on the networks, it is on billboards, and it is written on handmade signs in store windows. It is being sung by Congress members and by fans attending the first baseball games after the tragedy. Kids are praying in public classrooms. Churches are overflowing with people. The media broadcast Catholic masses, Protestant services, and ad hoc prayer gatherings around the country. People seem nice, kind, and more civil. NYC experienced no looting in the wake of the disaster, but instead experienced an outflowing of love and support for rescue workers. All of this provides hope—hope for a better America. America has the choice to turn the worst single day in American history into a revival of truth and spirituality in this country. Will it happen? I hope.

I hope the next time someone thinks of returning to a life of crime, murder, and/or robbery, he remembers the screams and cries of those watching the WTC tumble to the ground.

I hope the next time someone becomes mad at a neighbor for allowing his kids to run through his yard, he remembers our President fighting back tears when describing his reaction to this tragedy.

I hope the next time the National Anthem is played at a ballgame, a dad and his son will remove their caps and put their hands over their hearts, instead of dad checking his voicemail messages—remembering the firefighters at Ground Zero hoisting the American flag above the rubble.

I hope the next time our media thinks of broadcasting explicit and violent videos, movies, and TV shows aimed directly at our kids, they think first of the hundreds of children who have lost parents in this tragedy—parents who will not be there to protect their children from such filth.

I hope the next time someone thinks of uttering a racist joke or comment at another, he thinks of the multitudes of men and women, from all races and creeds, working as a human chain in the "bucket brigade" at Ground Zero—all working together to save lives.

I hope the next time a mother thinks of taking her end-of-week check to gambling riverboats instead of spending time with her children, she will instead think of the millions of dollars donated to the Red Cross and other agencies to assist those who suffered in these attacks.

I hope the next time someone thinks of shedding another's blood, he will instead remember the overwhelming blood donations around America toward the rescue and relief efforts.

I hope the next time an elderly person needs help and assistance, instead of walking by, someone will think of the two Morgan Stanley employees who carried an injured woman down sixty flights of the WTC.

I hope that the next time a father thinks of deserting his family, he thinks of the fathers who have been lost, and will never again get to hold and comfort their children.

I could go on. I hope and I pray that this tragedy will bring America to its knees—not in defeat, but in prayer. And as America rises up to a new tomorrow, I hope that Americans embrace the fruit of the spirit— love, joy, peace, patience, kindness, goodness, faithfulness, gentleness, and self-control.

I hope. . . .

Unfortunately, my letter was never published, but to my surprise and joy it has been forwarded to hundreds, if not thousands, of Americans by email. I have received emails from teachers, lawyers, World War II veterans, and others from all over America, claiming that my letter touched them in a profound way following the tragedies of September 11, 2001. Their responses provided the incentive for me to expand on the letter and to explore in more depth my hope for America.

Chapter I.

Fruit of the Spirit

I, like many Americans, have read Bruce Wilkinson's *The Prayer of Jabez* and *Secrets of the Vine*. Likewise, I have read Hank Hanegraaff's *The Prayer of Jesus*, which dissects each refrain of the Lord's Prayer in a profound manner, and helps us all to apply the prayer to our lives in a meaningful way. Any tool that can assist Christians in praying more effectively and in a more sincere and heartfelt manner is welcomed. However, the focus of this book is not to offer up a quick-fix prayer that claims to immediately change your life, but to ask you to consider how God wants *you* to change your life, consistent with scripture. Thus, I have chosen not to necessarily instruct you on how or when to pray, but instead I address how we should live our lives when not praying. In other words, how do we interact with those among us, both believers and non-believers, as we live the way that God has called us to live? How do we carry out God's plan for our lives, becoming shining lights to others of the love and compassion of Christ and what He can do in their lives? Of course, this book is by no means meant to replace your daily prayer time. Instead, my hope is that it will encourage you to add to your prayers a heartfelt request that God will give you the strength to apply the fruit of the spirit to your everyday existence.

A Christian pop-rock band, the Newsboys, declares in their song "Shine" that those who don't know Jesus are "on the outside looking bored." To the contrary, many in America think that Christians are a preachy, boring lot. The Newsboys declare that the opposite is true, and it is, for those who have truly turned their lives over to Christ and strive to emulate Him. How can Christians display an open love for Christ and for their families, friends, and others that would cause them to say, "Wow, Christians are fun and loving! How can I experience the joy and fulfillment Christians experience?"

Obviously, the Old Testament provides basic and fundamental rules for a civilized society, a society with God at its core. The Ten Commandments, although simple in word, provide a framework of laws that builds the foundation for any godly civilization. In fact, the basic tenets of our democracy, and of our laws, are derived from the absolute truths Moses set forth in Deuteronomy 5:7–21 and Exodus 20:3–17:

> You shall have no other gods before me.

> You shall not make for yourself an idol in the form of anything in heaven above or on the earth beneath or in the waters below. You shall not bow down to them or worship them; for I, the Lord your God, am a jealous God, punishing the children for the sin of the fathers to the third and fourth generation of those who hate me, but showing love to a thousand [generations] of those who love me and keep my commandments.

> You shall not misuse the name of the Lord your God, for the Lord will not hold anyone guiltless who mis-

uses his name.

Observe the Sabbath day by keeping it holy, as the Lord your God has commanded you. . . .

Honor your father and your mother, as the Lord your God has commanded you, so that you may live long and that it may go well with you in the land the Lord your God is giving you.

You shall not murder.

You shall not commit adultery.

You shall not steal.

You shall not give false testimony against your neighbor.

You shall not covet your neighbor's wife. You shall not set your desire on your neighbor's house or land, his manservant or maidservant, his ox or donkey, or anything that belongs to your neighbor.

Many of the Commandments address the very foundation of a civilized society, whether Biblically based or not. Do not lie, murder, steal, commit adultery, or covet others' belongings. Respect your father and mother. Most of the world's religions would be hard pressed to argue with these Old Testament tenets, notwithstanding zealots such as Osama Bin Laden, Hitler, David Koresh, Jim Jones, and others who over the course of human history have corrupted and twisted religion for their own diabolical and evil purposes.

For Christians, the Bible—and particularly the New

Testament—is chock full of additional instructions for godly living. However, I believe one simple passage in Galatians holds the promise of a spiritual renewal in this country more than any other. Like the Commandments, it is simple in word, but much harder in deed. Most of us do not struggle with many of the Commandments. We have not murdered, or committed adultery, or stolen material objects from others. However, we may have idolized rock stars, sports heroes, and others; we all have put other gods before Him, such as money, fame, power, and influence; and we can hardly get through a day without telling a host of white lies to our children and to our friends.

But Galatians 5:22, 23 provides much more than a set of basic rules for living. It is more than a "thou shalt not" instruction book with cut-and-dried tests of compliance. Instead, Paul's challenge in Galatians is a short guide for living that, although simple to state, is much harder to put into practice. I submit that if we try—if America tries—we may, in fact, subvert the very evil that has brought America to its knees in sorrow (and in prayer) and back to its feet in anger. In aspiring to the fruit of the spirit found in the following passage, we can strengthen America tenfold. In fact, if we truly adhere to the apostle Paul's plea in Galatians, we could hardly violate most of the Commandments: "But the fruit of the Spirit is love, joy, peace, patience, kindness, goodness, faithfulness, gentleness and self-control. Against such things there is no law" (Galatians 5:22, 23).

In Galatians 5, Paul pleads with the Galatians to embrace the fruit of the spirit. He cautions in Galatians 5:13 that the freedom purchased for us by Jesus Christ on the cross must not be used "to indulge the sinful nature; rather, serve one another in love." In Galatians 5:14, Paul continues by saying that "the entire law is summed up in a single command: 'Love your neighbor as yourself.'"

In the weeks following the September 11, 2001, attacks

on New York City and Washington, D.C., Americans appeared to heed Paul's command to "love your neighbor as yourself," although many did so unknowingly. Almost $1 billion was raised privately from Americans across our nation. Over $150 million was raised in an "America's Heroes" concert performance broadcast on thirty television networks and eight thousand radio stations across the globe, and the Red Cross was able to provide millions in direct assistance to victims' families. Was America heeding Paul's directive? Did Americans together read Galatians 5 and strive to harvest the fruit that had long been dormant in their busy lives? Were they heeding Christ's call to "love your neighbor as yourself"? I do not think all of America collectively and consciously has chosen to heed Paul's words, but something *is* different in America post-September 11, 2001. Now, how do we catch lightning in a bottle, heed Biblical truths, and reach our full potential, both individually and as a nation?

We can start by praying for our nation and seeking God's guidance. Consider 2 Chronicles 7:14: "If my people, who are called by my name, will humble themselves and pray and seek my face and turn from their wicked ways, then will I hear from heaven and will forgive their sin and will *heal their land*" (italics added).

We are living in a time of great uncertainty, but God promises to heal our land if we humble ourselves and pray, and seek to do God's will. America needs more than simply a time of grieving to heal from the September 11th attacks. America needs more than a few months of patriotic flag waving. My plea is that we not only grieve and display our patriotism, but that we heed God's words in 2 Chronicles, and that in seeking God's face and turning from wickedness, we embrace the fruit of the spirit. However, embracing the fruit of the spirit is not a short-term fix for our disappointment and despair surrounding September 11th, but instead is a spiritual playbook for lifelong living. In this book I strive to put these spiritual plays into action, and assist you in unlocking the fruit of the spirit in your life.

Chapter II.

Love

Love is patient, love is kind. It does not envy, it does not boast, it is not proud. It is not rude, it is not self-seeking, it is not easily angered, it keeps no record of wrongs. Love does not delight in evil but rejoices with the truth. (1 Corinthians 13:4–6)

Love is likely the most overused word in American society. "I love the Cleveland Browns!" "I love chocolate!" "I love my new car!" Americans use the word "love" for everything ranging from their feelings of simply liking something—even a material object—to deep emotional caring for God or one's spouse or children. In fact, no word permeates the New Testament more than the word "love." Paul rightfully first mentions love in Galatians 5:22, and likewise love is a focal point of this book. All other fruit naturally flow from love. Kindness, goodness, joy, peace, etc.—they all flow from a love of God, spouse, kids, friends, family, and one another. 1 Corinthians 13, a passage often quoted at weddings, beautifully sums up the importance God places on love:

> If I speak in the tongues of men and of angels, but have not love, I am only a resounding gong or a clanging cymbal.
>
> If I have the gift of prophecy and can fathom all mysteries and all knowledge, and if I have a faith that can move mountains, but have not love, I am nothing. If I give all I possess to the poor and surrender my body to the flames, but have not love, I gain nothing.
>
> Love is patient, love is kind. It does not envy, it does not boast, it is not proud. It is not rude, it is not self-seeking, it is not easily angered, it keeps no record of wrongs. Love does not delight in evil but rejoices with the truth. It always protects, always trusts, always hopes, always perseveres.
>
> Love never fails. . . . And now these three remain: faith, hope and love. ***But the greatest of these is love.*** (Italics added)

What a beautiful definition of true love! This passage for me is another affirmation that the Bible is truly God-breathed. Think of the context in which this was written almost two thousand years ago. Women in such times were not treated as equal partners and were clearly beneath men in virtually every society on earth, including Jewish society. In light of this, Paul offers up a definition and call to love that is literally inspired by God. It is difficult for us in the twenty-first century to fathom or to live up to the call in Corinthians even as we are bombarded with books, videos, and other information on how to be better fathers, mothers, husbands, wives, parents, children, friends, etc. I wonder how men in particular reacted to Paul's sensitive and caring description of love at the time he wrote this letter to the Corinthians.

God's Love

How do we really know when someone truly loves us in the way Christ loved the church? Does God love us? How can we love and be loved? What is true love?

First and foremost, God loves us. God's great love for us is summed up in offering His own Son's life for us, so that we may, if we so freely choose, enter into a personal relationship with the Son and the Father, and may accept God's great gift of eternal life. Has there ever been a greater sacrifice, or a greater expression of love? God offered up his own Son, who was freē of sin, to take our place and pay for our failures so that we could attain eternal life: "For God so loved the world that he gave his one and only Son, that whoever believes in him shall not perish but have eternal life. For God did not send his Son into the world to condemn the world, but to save the world through him" (John 3:16, 17).

Our ability to truly love others in the full and complete way that only God intended for us must start with our love of God and acceptance of His Son as our savior. Consider Jesus' direct and clear claim that salvation comes only through a relationship with Him: "I am the way and the truth and the life. No one comes to the Father except through me. If you really knew me, you would know my Father as well" (John 14:6, 7). The Apostle John also explains in 1 John that God's love for us begins and ends with our acknowledgment that Jesus is His Son, and that the door to God's supreme love for us is opened only by first accepting Christ:

> If *anyone acknowledges that Jesus is the Son of God, God lives in him and he in God.* And so we know and rely on the love God has for us. *God is love.* Whoever

lives in love lives in God, and God in him. In this way, *love is made complete among us* so that we will have confidence on the day of judgment, because in this world we are like him. There is no fear in love. But *perfect love drives out fear*, because fear has to do with punishment. The one who fears is not made perfect in love. *We love because he first loved us.* (1 John 4:15–19, italics added)

Can it be stated more simply than "God is love"? Read these passages again, carefully and slowly. Once we accept Christ, God then lives within us and we live within God. Since God is in fact synonymous with love, our love is then complete. Once we experience God's true and unabashed love, our fear is driven away, and we, in turn, are then able to truly love others as God intended for us to love. Consider also Paul's words in Romans 8:38, 39: "For I am convinced that neither death nor life, neither angels nor demons, neither the present nor the future, nor any powers, neither height nor depth, *nor anything else in all creation, will be able to separate us from the love of God that is in Christ Jesus* our Lord" (italics added).

In essence, we are able to love God by first following Christ, and once we experience God's love through Christ, nothing else "in all creation" will be able to separate us from God's love. Through Christ, we establish a personal relationship with God, and once that relationship is established, we can then realize just how beautiful, wonderful, powerful, magnificent, bright, just, joyous, and awesome God truly is.

God's love is bottomless. He made us in His image, and we were, in turn, created to love and to worship Him. You have likely heard the phrase "love the sinner, but hate the sin." God will continue to love us even when we fall short of His expectations for us, because He expects that we will fail. God is faithful: "Know therefore that the Lord your God is

God; he is the faithful God, keeping his covenant of love to a thousand generations of those who love him and keep his commands. . . . If you pay attention to these laws and are careful to follow them, then the Lord your *God will keep his covenant of love with you*, as he swore to your forefathers" (Deuteronomy 7:9, 12, italics added). In turn, we must respond to God's love with love for Him, and try our very best to live as He would have us live. Deuteronomy 10:12 states, "And now, O Israel, what does the Lord your God ask of you but to fear the Lord your God, to *walk in all his ways, to love him, to serve the Lord your God with all your heart and with all your soul*" (italics added).

Some may have to overcome fortified mental obstacles to accept God's love. I had a verbally abusive, alcoholic father as a child. I was ten and my sister was seven when he mercifully moved out and my parents divorced. He worked as a salesman for a pharmaceutical company, so he was always traveling and was rarely home during the week. I can't remember more than once or twice when he ever shot a basketball with me, threw a football with me, helped me with homework, or even read a book to me. Most of the time when he wasn't working, he was at the track or out getting drunk, but when he was home, our house was packed with tension. As a result, most of my early childhood was a blur. I spent a lot of time playing alone, especially when my father was home. I was terrified of him. His booming, cursing voice permeated our household virtually every day he was there. It was a living hell. To this day I cannot tolerate anyone who yells, screams, or attempts to intimidate others. Such bullying tactics raise my ire quicker than almost anything. As a result, I have attempted to take the exact opposite tact with my children. I want them to grow up in a loving, nurturing, safe, and happy home, free from the concerns I had as a child.

Growing up in this type of situation, I questioned whether

I deserved fatherly love, or could ever truly accept fatherly love from another. I believe many in America carry similar or much worse burdens, buried deep inside them. Many times our defenses are so deeply ingrained in our very persona that we may forget the true roots of our defensive attitudes and actions toward those who truly do try to love us. For many, those same defenses are raised to resist God and His faithful call. Although difficult to overcome, if we can lower our shields, knock on Christ's door, and then unconditionally accept Him into our hearts and our lives, we can become reunited with God and experience His unparalleled Fatherly love. Once back safely in His arms, we can then begin to love others in the way that God calls us to love, and accept love from others.

When we sincerely love others, such as those in our families, we try our very best not to disappoint them or fall short of their expectations for us. People innately strive to apply the fruit of the spirit to these loving relationships, even if they are not Christians. And we forgive those we love when they honestly admit their wrongs and sincerely apologize for their actions. God is no different. God expects us to apply the fruit of the spirit to our relationship with Him and to not leave Him with the leftovers of our lives. Loving God with all one's heart and soul is much more than a once-a-week church service. It connotes a deep personal relationship with Christ that is grounded in our realization of God's great expression of love for us. Again, our charge to love God and to develop a meaningful and personal relationship with Him cannot be overstated. It is the key to unlocking our ability to truly love others, and to unlocking the fruit of the spirit within us.

Love One Another

In Luke 10:25–28, when Jesus was asked by an expert in the law "what must I do to inherit eternal life?" He asked the man, "What is written in the Law?" and the expert answered, "'Love the Lord your God with all your heart and with all your soul and with all your strength and with all your mind'; and, 'Love your neighbor as yourself.'" Jesus then told him he had answered correctly. Therefore, when asked the phenomenally important question of how to inherit eternal life, Jesus commanded him, and every believer, to do two things: to first love God with all of his heart, soul, strength, and mind; and to love his neighbor. When asked to elaborate as to who is one's neighbor, Jesus told the well-known parable of the Good Samaritan. According to Jesus, everyone— friend or stranger—is your neighbor.

God knows our failures before we fail. We fail repeatedly to love one another. He knows we cannot always measure up, and He will always forgive us if we genuinely confess our failures, but He does not permit us to stop *trying* to measure up. In 1 John 5–10, John clearly states that we will continue to fall short of God's expectations for us even after we accept Christ, but he also cautions against denying our wrongs before God. He states:

> God is light; in him there is no darkness at all. If we claim to have fellowship with him yet walk in the darkness, we lie and do not live by the truth. But if we walk in the light, as he is in the light, we have fellowship with one another, and the blood of Jesus, his Son, purifies us from all sin. If we claim to be without sin, we deceive ourselves and the truth is not in us. If we confess our sins, he is faithful and just and will forgive us our sins and purify us from all unrighteousness. If we claim we have not sinned, we make him out to be a liar and his word has no place in our lives.

We all sin, but true confession, and an honest desire to turn from sin, will enable us to walk in the light and not in the darkness. God asks only that we constantly strive to do better, and when we falter, that we confess, receive His forgiveness, and strive again to do what is right. The focus in 1 John is that we not *continue* to sin or *repeat* our sins. We all sin, but to repeat the identical sins over and over makes a mockery of God's love, compassion, and forgiveness. If we do not attempt to overcome our failings, and instead continue to disobey God, our actions speak louder than our words. For example, how are God and His message viewed when a self-proclaimed Christian marriage counselor or pastor, who preaches on fidelity, doesn't "practice what he preaches"? The good news of Christianity is dealt a severe blow in the eyes of those who witness such hypocrisy. This does not mean we must live perfect lives, but we must strive to do what is right. "I can do everything through him who gives me strength" (Philippians 4:13). "Never tire of doing what is right" (2 Thessalonians 3:13).

John also reiterates Jesus' most important commandment to love one another. He goes further, saying that "whoever loves his brother lives in the light, and there is nothing in him to make him stumble" (1 John 2:10). In contrast, to hate your brother is to walk in darkness and remain separated from God. In fact, John states that "anyone who does not love remains in death" (1 John 3:14). Thus, deep, caring, and compassionate love is the centerpiece of salvation and a full and complete life. One really does not even live without love.

God loves us in just such a manner, and as discussed above, we should also love God completely with *all* of our being. As God's love pours into and through us, His love will be revealed in our dealings with others. If we invite God to reside within our hearts and guide our actions, we can do nothing but glorify Him in how we treat others. "If you really keep the royal law found in Scripture, 'Love your neighbor as yourself,' you are doing right" (James 2:8).

When we lose sight of God's love and His commandments, we err and fall short of His expectations for us. The good news is that we are not destined for separation from God. Our true love for God is manifested through our honest confession to God of our misdeeds, and our saving grace is God's promise of forgiveness and purification from our sins through Christ.

God knows we will face untold temptations in life, but He is a constant encourager. Faith is a choice. God provides us with the tools to fight what is wrong, but we are not robots. He made us free—free to hate, but free also to love. This freedom in choosing to love is what brings us immeasurable joy. Otherwise, upon what frame of reference could we judge love or joy? Only when we freely choose the proper course, with God's guidance, rather than walk in darkness filled with hatred, envy, and greed, do we see how wonderful the light, and love, can be. Stark contrasts reveal beautiful, true love. What have you done lately to show that you love others? Have you treated your neighbor as you would yourself? In later chapters, I will explore how our love is manifested further in our dealings with others.

Husbands and Wives

No earthly relationship is more sacred before God than that of husband and wife. Obviously, thousands of pages have been devoted to the husband-wife relationship, and I do not profess to summarize all of such good advice in this book. But, in addition to the call to love in 1 Corinthians set forth above, in Ephesians 5:21–33, husbands and wives are commanded to "submit to one another out of reverence for Christ":

> Wives, submit to your husbands as to the Lord. For the husband is the head of the wife as Christ is the head of the church, his body, of which he is the Savior. Now as the church submits to Christ, so also wives should sub-

mit to their husbands in everything.

Husbands, love your wives, just as Christ loved the
church and gave himself up for her to make her holy,
cleansing her by the washing with water through the
word, and to present her to himself as a radiant church,
without stain or wrinkle or any other blemish, but holy
and blameless.
In this same way, husbands ought to love their wives as
their own bodies. He who loves his wife loves himself.
After all, no one ever hated his own body, but he feeds
and cares for it, just as Christ does the church—for we
are members of his body.
"For this reason a man will leave his father and mother
and be united to his wife, and the two will become one
flesh."

This is a profound mystery—but I am talking about
Christ and the church. However, each one of you also
must love his wife as he loves himself, and the wife
must respect her husband.

Much has been made of the "submission" theme of this
passage, but I instead think the primary focus of this passage
is not on the submission of a wife to her husband, but on the
charge to husbands to love their wives as Christ loved the
church. What an awesome charge to keep! How can husbands truly treat their wives with the respect, reverence,
love, patience, kindness, and gentleness that Christ
bestowed on the church? Again, God expects us to fail, but
He also, as stated in 1 John above, expects us to strive to
walk in the light and to avoid darkness.

Men are also challenged to love their wives as they love
themselves. Again, this is an enormous challenge for most
men. Men are inherently selfish, and are much more so than

most women. A man wants "his" time on the golf course, "his" time with his buddies, or "his" time in front of the television. The Bible asks men to love their wives as much as themselves. Therefore, a wife's personal time is as important, or more so, than her husband's. A wife's thoughts, feelings, desires, and dreams should be of equal weight in a husband's eyes as his own.

Many men would be appalled at my next statement, but I truly believe that ninety percent of the world's problems are caused by men who fail to heed God's call to truly love their wives (and children) as Christ loved the church. Much of the unfaithfulness, loneliness, disrespect, arguments, and simple neglect in marriages today could be eliminated if men lived up to their responsibilities as commanded by God. The Bible contains adequate warnings to men, and they are obviously necessary given the well-documented failures of men—failures that have drastic consequences on women, children, and society at large:

> Husbands, love your wives and do not be harsh with them. (Colossians 3:19)

> Husbands, in the same way be considerate as you live with your wives, and treat them with respect. . . . (1 Peter 3:7)

> If anyone does not provide for his relatives, and especially for his immediate family, he has denied the faith and is worse than an unbeliever. (1 Timothy 5:8)

Women are not so frequently warned and chastised in the Bible. Instead, God understands the inherent selfish nature of men, and spends a great deal of time pleading with them to act responsibly. Again, my father is a classic example of how a man can choose to follow his ego, ambition, and selfish and destructive desires, and severely damage his marriage and relationship with his children. My father never loved my mother in a Christ-like way, and he never loved and cared for his children in the way the Father cares for us. He instead focused exclusively on his own selfish interests, which inflicted severe emotional and financial damage on his family that has not dissipated to this day. More on selfish "love" later.

Parental Love

As parents, our desire to love and protect our children is analogous to God's love for us. In 1 Timothy 5:8, God calls us to care and provide for our families, and particularly our immediate families. How great does God consider this responsibility? The one who neglects his family is "denied the faith and is worse than an unbeliever." Why would God withdraw salvation from those who neglect, desert, or fail to provide for their families? Well, consider how God has provided for and will provide for our every need:

> Therefore I tell you, do not worry about your life, what you will eat or drink; or about your body, what you will wear. Is not life more important than food, and the body more important than clothes? Look at the birds of the air; they do not sow or reap or store away in barns, and yet your heavenly Father feeds them. Are you not much more valuable than they? (Matthew 6:25–27)

Jesus asks us not to worry about our needs—God will meet those needs, since He obviously values and cares for us more than for mere birds. This obviously does not mean that God will fulfill our every want or desire, but He will meet our true needs. What we "need" in our prosperous America is a subject of great debate. I doubt that God's view and our view of true needs are aligned.

The same is true with our children. They believe they "need" the newest video game console, a new bike, a tenth Barbie, etc. The point is that God our Father provides for us just as earthly fathers and mothers should provide for their children—not spoiling them, but meeting their needs. God does not promise Christians great wealth, power, and fame, and He knows better than we do what is best for us. Consider the Lord's Prayer:

> Our Father in heaven, hallowed be your name, your kingdom come, your will be done on earth as it is in heaven. Give us today our daily bread. Forgive us our debts, as we also have forgiven our debtors. And lead us not into temptation, but deliver us from the evil one. (Matthew 6:9–13)

Notice that Jesus commanded us to ask God that "*your* will be done," not that "*our*" will or desire be done. Note also that we ask not that God will give us what we want or deserve, but what we truly need—"our daily bread." We do not have to buy our children's love with material possessions, just as God does not buy our love and obedience with promises that faith in Him will bring great riches and a carefree life. God, in fact, warns us that we will face great tribulations as Christians. Instead, we are called to provide for our families' true needs—emotionally, spiritually, and financially—and emulate God's great example of love, sacrifice, and provision for us in our relationships with our families.

Consider again my father and his failings. Do you know a father consumed by his job, working sixty hours a week and rarely spending time with his kids? Do you know a coward who has deserted his or her family? Do you know a "deadbeat dad"? Are you a "deadbeat dad"? Is it hard to imagine why Paul's words are so direct and stern with regard to one's duty to provide for his or her family? As stated previously, each fruit of the spirit is divinely intertwined with the others. I will present more on family responsibilities later.

Selfish "Love"

I began this chapter with examples of different material and earthly possessions or other things that we profess to "love." Interestingly, John uses the word "love" to prove a point about what in fact is *not* love, and what we should not love: "Do not love the world or anything in the world. If anyone loves the world, the love of the Father is not in him. For everything in the world—the cravings of sinful man, the lust of his eyes and the boasting of what he has and does—comes not from the Father but from the world" (1 John 2:15, 16).

The focus on "me" highlighted in these verses is really just "love" of oneself—selfishness. This is not the love Paul so eloquently and passionately describes in his first letter to the Corinthians. In addition, John warns us of boasting, lusting and coveting another's possessions, and craving selfish desires. Wow, don't these Biblical warnings go right to the heart of America's obsession with sex and consumerism? John pleads with us to fight the love of the "world" and its temptations. The world he speaks of is one of instant gratification—"get it now—no payments for a year"; wait on nothing—you "deserve" a new car, room of furniture or wardrobe, even if you can't afford it; you deserve a "happy" life with no boundaries, no rules, and no concern for your actions on others.

With all of our freedoms come incredible temptations. Nowhere in the world are people more free than in America, but nowhere is there more crime, divorce, abuse, and drug use. Why? Again, God expects us to fail, but He also desires that we admit our failures, receive forgiveness, and stand whole once again, striving to please Him. It is impossible to refrain from sin, but only with God's help can one truly live in the light and overcome our inherent selfishness. Paul gives us hope that we can defeat our temptations: "No temptation has seized you except what is common to man. And God is faithful; he will not let you be tempted beyond what you can bear. But when you are tempted, he will also provide a way out so that you can stand up under it" (1 Corinthians 10:13).

Obviously, this passage does not apply just to money, but to all worldly temptations. Paul states what we now know— that you cannot defeat worldly temptations without faith in God, and that God will not let us be tempted beyond what we can bear. However, inner strength alone is not enough to overcome temptation. We must call upon God to "lead us not into temptation" and to strengthen our resolve to walk in the light.

Love of money and wealth is addressed in both the Old and New Testaments hundreds of times. I believe if the Bible had been written in modern times, warnings about worshipping the god of money would be mentioned even more extensively. Contrasted with the definition of a "rich" man in Biblical times, I dare say that Jesus would have directed his words in Matthew 19:23, 24 to virtually all of modern day America—"I tell you the truth, it is hard for a rich man to enter the kingdom of heaven. Again I tell you, it is easier for a camel to go through the eye of a needle than for a rich man to enter the kingdom of God." Are material possessions and wealth inherently evil? No, but "love" of money and obsession with accumulation of wealth is a sin. What then can we do to cleanse our hearts, get off the treadmill to the "American Dream," and focus our hearts on true love?

Dozens of Christian books have been written about money and its potential evils. I do not attempt to reiterate all of such great advice here. However, true Biblical love, as I have described above, can be overcome by a false love of money and obsession with accumulating wealth. Biblical advice regarding money and wealth is stern and direct.

Jesus even used the words "watch out" to gain our attention when cautioning us about greed and our focus on material possessions: "Watch out! Be on your guard against all kinds of greed; a man's life does not consist in the abundance of his possessions. . . . This is how it will be with anyone who stores up things for himself but is not rich toward God" (Luke 12:15, 21).

Jesus warns us that the key to happiness is not our possessions. "For where your treasure is, there your heart will be also" (Luke 12:34). In other words, "No servant can serve two masters. Either he will hate the one and love the other, or he will be devoted to the one and despise the other. You cannot serve both God and Money" (Luke 16:13). Money is an insatiable beast that has the power to sap your energies and subvert God's place in your life and in your heart. We can become enslaved to money. Material possessions offer the perception of power and importance, but great wealth can be made, and lost, in an instant. Just ask the thousands of once dot com millionaires who are now looking for jobs. Money makes promises that cannot be kept and promises happiness that is fleeting and superficial.

America may just have survived as the longest-running free civilization and democracy on earth because it was founded on Christian values. God has bestowed phenomenal blessings on America, so why has it taken such a tragic event to wake us up to Biblical truths? And, even when we know such truths, why is it so difficult to adhere to them? The apostle Paul in 1 Timothy seeks to help Timothy (and us) deal with the issue of contentment and the temptation of riches: "But godliness with contentment is great gain. For we brought nothing into the world, and we can take nothing out of it. But if we have food and clothing, we will be content with that. People who want to get rich fall into temptation and a trap and into many foolish and harmful desires that plunge men into ruin and destruction. For the love of money is a root of all kinds of evil. Some people, eager for money, have wandered from the faith and pierced themselves with many griefs" (1 Timothy 6:6–10).

Our love of money and our obsession with the "American Dream" can drive a wedge between God and us. However, many of us believe that we can serve two masters. Juggling priorities is a constant and daily struggle, and nowhere in the world is the gospel of consumerism preached more than in modern-day America. From birth, the rat race accumulation of possessions is preached as the one and only way to "success." To refuse to participate in this unwinnable race is tantamount to treason. When two-thirds of the American economy is driven by the combined purchasing power of individual Americans, it becomes almost our patriotic duty to earn more, spend more, and "enjoy" more. Hey, we deserve it, right? But, when will we learn? Paul states the obvious in 1 Timothy—we cannot take our possessions with us. We brought nothing into the world, and we can take nothing out of it. The message is so simple and so true, yet many times we don't realize it until it is too late.

I have spoken to countless people who have sacrificed their faith, their families, and their marriages to climb the corporate ladder, to become partners at their law firms or accounting firms, or to put their very heart and soul into their new business ventures only to remain unfulfilled. Others may have mentally made the jump off the treadmill, but they never have had heart-to-heart talks with their spouses for fear that a diminished standard of living would be unthinkable. If this book is speaking to you, maybe your spouse and your kids only wish they had you, and not the weak substitute for a husband, wife, mommy, or daddy that wealth can purchase. Don't wait until the new car smell has worn off, the country club dues become unmanageable, the new dress becomes tattered, and/or the kids are off to college to realize what you may lose—time, family, and contentment. Consider Paul's "secret" to contentment in Philippians 4:11–13: "I am not saying this because I am in need, for I have *learned to be content whatever the circumstances*. I know what it is to be in need, and I know what it is to have plenty. *I have learned the secret of being content in any and every situation, whether well fed or hungry, whether living in plenty or in want. I can do everything through him who gives me strength*" (italics added).

Talking to other men, reading books such as Patrick Morley's *The Man in the Mirror*, and participating in men's Bible studies led me in 2000 to leave a lucrative position at an international law firm for an in-house legal position with a corporation headquartered in Cincinnati. I thought I could serve two masters—God and my earthly master (money/my boss). I grew up in a very modest household, and by the age of 33 I earned four times what my mother earned as a schoolteacher at age 58. I had two wonderful small children, a beautiful wife, an incredible house and nice cars, and absolutely no life. I thought I could have it all—the American Dream—without any sacrifices. I quickly learned that God led me to such a prestigious law firm, with a phenomenal salary, office, and influence, so I could realize that I had "won," but had really lost. I had achieved a financial and perceived notion of success that most in America would envy. But, I had won nothing but fifteen-hour days, a cell phone attached to my ear at all hours of the night and day, unyielding stress, and a few more toys. I had been a Christian for years at the time, and (when home) I gave every waking moment to my wife and kids, but I was kidding myself. I finally realized that I could not balance my work, family and faith in the manner in which I felt God calling me. Three Biblical passages drove home the point for me that my workaholic lifestyle in dogged pursuit of worldly success was misplaced.

The first is Deuteronomy 8:17–19, which reminds us that

only God gives us the talent to earn our money and develop wealth. If we bow down before the god of money and claim that we, and we alone, have earned and deserve our wealth, we will surely not inherit God's kingdom: "You may say to yourself, 'My power and the strength of my hands have produced this wealth for me.' But remember the Lord your God, for it is he who gives you the ability to produce wealth, and so confirms his covenant, which he swore to your forefathers, as it is today. If you ever forget the Lord your God and follow other gods and worship and bow down to them, I testify against you today that you will surely be destroyed."

The second is James 1:22–25, which commands us to obey God's word, particularly when we fully understand what God is calling us to do. Look in the mirror. Do you like what you see? Is God speaking to you through the scriptures, or through this book today, pleading with you to change your destructive ways? Do you know the path you must follow, but continue to turn in the wrong direction? In simple terms, "knowing is not doing": "Do not merely listen to the word, and so deceive yourselves. *Do what it says.* Anyone who listens to the word but does not do what it says is like a man who looks at his face in a mirror and, after looking at himself, goes away and immediately forgets what he looks like. But the man who looks intently into the perfect law that gives freedom, and continues to do this, *not forgetting what he has heard, but doing it—he will be blessed in what he does*" (italics added).

Finally, Ecclesiastes 5:10, 11 warns us of bowing to the insatiable appetite and love of money, and of its ramifications, with unyielding clarity: "Whoever loves money never has money enough; whoever loves wealth is never satisfied with his income. This too is meaningless. As goods increase, so do those who consume them. And what benefit are they to the owner except to feast his eyes on them?" It is hard to believe these passages are two thousand years old! Their words ring so true that they could have been found on last Sunday morning's editorial page. I beg you to heed God's word on this issue.

As you know, the Bible obviously does not condemn a drive to do one's best and to work hard and honestly, whether in school, work or at home. Consider Jesus' parable of the talents and the "wicked, lazy servant" in Matthew 25:14–26 (and in Chapter VI – Kindness and Goodness). Work is to be a blessing and a joy, a gift from God. We are to use our God-given talents wisely. Likewise, the fruits of our labor are to be enjoyed. Remember, "It is good and proper for a man to eat and drink, and to find satisfaction in his toilsome labor under the sun during the few days of life God has given him—for this is his lot. Moreover, when God gives any man wealth and possessions, and enables him to enjoy them, to accept his lot and be happy in his work—this is a gift of God" (Ecclesiastes 5:18, 19).

Wealth and possessions are not evil, so long as we do not obsess over them. Enjoy what God has provided to you and to your family—it is a "gift from God"—and be a faithful steward over God's blessings for you. However, the Bible does condemn a workaholic lifestyle fueled by a hyper-ambitious desire for self-importance, pride and accumulation of wealth and possessions no matter the costs. I know. Such a desire once consumed me, and in turn, my family.

If you had not been clearly warned of the sinful grip of materialism before reading this chapter, do not tarry now. The wonderful news of the Bible is that anyone, no matter what his predisposition or desires, can choose the right path, and with God's help and God's love, can establish and maintain a balanced work life, marriage, and family life with God at the core. The sad truth is that too many people in America and beyond never humble themselves before God, and therefore never reach their full potential in the eyes of God. As a result, their marriages and relationships with family and friends are never properly in focus. The focus is instead on "me" and not on serving God and others. You may have heard the phrase "And Marriage Makes Three." A poem by this name is framed on my bedroom wall. A marriage and family life with the fruit of the spirit at the core can never be achieved without a deep and heartfelt love for God and His son Jesus Christ.

Chapter III.

Joy

An angel of the Lord appeared to them, and the glory of the Lord shone around them, and they were terrified. But the angel said to them, "Do not be afraid. I bring you good news of great joy that will be for all the people. Today in the town of David a Savior has been born to you; he is Christ the Lord. (Luke 2:9–11)

In America today, most would describe "joy" as watching one's baby being born, seeing a daughter score her first soccer goal, earning a 100 on a test, saying "I do" to one's spouse, or watching a beloved alma mater win the NCAA basketball championship. Obviously, there is nothing wrong with enjoying such things in life. They are the some of the wonderful moments that make up one's earthly life.

In the Bible, joy is continually associated with a feeling of utter amazement and happiness associated with a true love of God. As Luke stated above, the greatest joy is the everlasting life offered by Christ. In almost every instance the word "joy" is used in the Bible, it connotes singing, shouting, and proclaiming a feeling deep in one's heart—

one that can be truly fulfilled only by a love of God. Joy is mentioned dozens of times in Psalms and Proverbs. The following verses are samples: "The Lord is my strength and my shield; my heart trusts in him, and I am helped. My heart leaps for joy and I will give thanks to him in song" (Psalm 28:7). "You love righteousness and hate wickedness; therefore God, your God, has set you above your companions by anointing you with the oil of joy (Psalm 45:7).

Many people would not equate obedience—whether to God or to one's parents, football coach, or boss—with joy. Many shun authority and rules at all costs. They claim that following Christ puts them in a box and places undue rules and restrictions on their freedom. On the surface, that may appear to be the case. As discussed previously, the Ten Commandments contain a fair number of "thou shalt nots." However, as evidenced by the fruit of the spirit, once the Holy Spirit resides within you, and your fruit is cultivated, true living really begins. Jesus claims that our joy will be complete only if we obey His commands and those of the Father: "If you obey my commands, you will remain in my love, just as I have obeyed my Father's commands and remain in his love. I have told you this so that my joy may be in you and that your joy may be complete. My command is this: Love each other as I have loved you" (John 15:10–12).

Jesus asks us to obey and trust God, and His love will then reveal itself in unabashed joy. By obeying, we remain in Jesus' love and in God's love so that "our joy may be complete." But how can such obedience result in a feeling of joy? We exhibit joy by loving God and others, and by acting out such love. The honesty and forgiveness that encompasses a true relationship with God can wash away feelings of inadequacy and shame, and replace them with love and joy. Once this loving relationship with God is established, the Holy Spirit will guide your actions and others will see your joy. "Be joyful always" (1 Thessalonians 5:16). Outward expressions of love show the world, and convey to the world, the joy in following Christ. Who hasn't experienced such joy in lending a helping hand to others in need, whether a friend, colleague, family member or stranger? Most of the time we are more fulfilled by our act of service than is the recipient of our service or gift.

Unfortunately, the mundane, everyday crises of our busy lives seek to rob us of joy. Life is full of meetings, laundry, gossip, worry, and disappointments. However, Jesus said, "Who of you by worrying can add a single hour to his life?" (Matthew 6:27). In fact, Jesus spoke often of worrying, which robs us of joy.

> Therefore I tell you, do not worry about your life, what you will eat or drink; or about your body, what you will wear. Is not life more important than food, and the body more important than clothes? Look at the birds of the air; they do not sow or reap or store away in barns, and yet your heavenly Father feeds them. Are you not much more valuable than they? Who of you by worrying can add a single hour to his life? And why do you worry about clothes? See how the lilies of the field grow. They do not labor or spin. Yet I tell you that not even Solomon in all his splendor was dressed like one of these. If that is how God clothes the grass of the field, which is here today and tomorrow is thrown into the fire, will he not much more clothe you, O you of little faith? So do not worry, saying, 'What shall we eat?' or 'What shall we drink?' or 'What shall we wear?' For the pagans run after all these things, and your heavenly Father knows that you need them. But seek first his kingdom and his righteousness, and all these things will be given to you as well. (Matthew 6:25–33)

Jesus commands us to focus not on our everyday existence—our clothes, food, or material possessions. Instead, He pleads with us not to worry of such things. But, in America today, that is much easier said than done. From the time we are children, we are programmed for consumerism (see "Love" above)—to want the latest toy, the newest sugar cereal (with prize), the newest video game, etc. As adults, our toys become more expensive—the new luxury car, the house we can't afford, or the vacation we deserve. We all struggle with the balance between the secular world in which we live and the spiritual world in which God asks us to focus our energies. Again, "Do not love the world or anything in the world. If anyone loves the world, the love of the Father is not in him" (1 John 2:15). Our ability to balance our energies and our focus between our worldly responsibilities and lives is made easier if we see such responsibilities through the proper perspectives.

Money, lust, greed, power, and manipulation of others bring only superficial happiness, not true Biblical joy. The landscape is littered with those who admittedly have pursued something or someone other than God, thinking that it would produce happiness and contentment. The promise is empty. How many examples of the fallen must we see to heed God's word—NFL heroes turned to prisoners due to drugs or promiscuity, televangelists and politicians who have lost their families pursuing the new and youngest office skirt, or mothers obsessed with their kids to the point that their marriages fall apart? Such obsession with something or someone becomes a true "love" and replaces God in our hearts. Our "happiness" eventually fades, leaving us empty and broken.

Don't get me wrong. As discussed in the previous chapter on "Love", God also allows us and calls us to experience joy in earthly pleasures. He has provided to us a fruitful and bountiful world for our enjoyment. Consider again Ecclesiastes 5:18, 19: "When God gives any man wealth and possessions, and enables him to enjoy them, to accept his lot and be happy in his work—this is a gift of God". Another example is when Luke speaks of Zechariah and Elizabeth, the parents of John the Baptist, being filled with joy upon the birth of John. Elizabeth was believed to be barren, so you can imagine the joy she and Zechariah experienced when an angel declared that not only would they have a son, but that he would be great in the sight of the Lord. What a wonderful joy! "He will be a joy and delight to you, and many will rejoice because of his birth, for he will be great in the sight of the Lord" (Luke 1:14, 15).

Even our work should be a joy. Work? How can work be joyful? Don't we work to make ends meet? Isn't work the punishment from being banished from the Garden of Eden? God begs to differ. Why would such a large portion of our lives be devoted to work if it were not a godly endeavor? Work can be tough and can cause many trials and heartaches, especially when we work to achieve the unreachable "American Dream." If we work solely for our own desires, and not those of our family and God, we join in a race that has no end and has no winner. However, God commands us to work with joy and without burden: "Obey your leaders and submit to their authority. They keep watch over you as men who must give an account. Obey them so that their work will be a joy, not a burden, for that would be of no advantage to you (Hebrews 13:17).

In fact, trials and difficulties in work and in life are clearly equated with joy in the Bible. For example, we read in James 1:2, 3: "Consider it pure joy, my brothers, whenever you face trials of many kinds, because you know that the testing of your faith develops perseverance." This sounds so contrary to our never-ending quest for "happiness" in America. We don't want "trials of many kinds." How can difficulties and problems strengthen us? How can they strengthen our faith in God? Trials that test our faith seem like the opposite of joy.

However, consider the Apostle Paul, or Chuck Colson, a convicted felon, or others you may know who had to essentially reach the depths of hopelessness before reaching for a lifeline from God. *Secrets of the Vine* focuses on this "pruning" of our sinful tendencies and our unproductive parts such that our godly fruit can grow. Many times one cannot know or experience true joy until one knows or experiences true despair.

Since September 11, 2001, why are so many people hugging their children more tightly, telling family members they love them, and thanking God for their lives and their families? Why do people worry less today that the house has not been swept? Why does the "small stuff," which burdened people prior to September 11, 2001, seem so meaningless to their lives today? They see misery on their television sets every day. They read about it. They may only now experience the joy of their children because they fear losing them. Recent world events do test our faith, but why do we continue to return to faith in such times? As the passage from James above so simply states, our faith may be tested by such trials, but we persevere. President Bush has spoken often of "America's resolve" in the war against terrorism. I believe this resolve equates to the perseverance spoken of in James. We mourn, cry, and ache for the victims of these acts of terror, but we pick ourselves up, dust ourselves off, fly our American flags, donate our time and money, love our neighbors, and defend our families and our nation with a renewed and stronger faith. In other words, we persevere.

Unfortunately, many times we take so much of what has been given to us for granted. We worry about the next promotion, the invitation to the next party, or our clothes not matching the latest fashion. Our ability to experience joy is buried in worry and clutter. We waltz over so many things every day that should bring us great joy, but a new couch, a new wardrobe, or a piece of chocolate candy will not do so. Such short-lived happiness is not true joy. Our relationship with God, our relationships with friends and family, and the giving of ourselves to others (i.e., service) bring us true joy and meaningful, lasting happiness.

Chapter IV.

Peace

Peace I leave with you; my peace I give you. I do not
give to you as the world gives. Do not let your hearts
be troubled and do not be afraid. (John 14:27)

The events of September 11th and their aftermath shat-
tered Americans' peace. Many times we think of peace
as the antithesis of war or fighting, and in many ways that is
true. However, peace means so much more in our lives than
simply the absence of war and physical confrontation. Most
importantly, God wants our hearts to be at peace and to be
free of fear, troubles, and worry. We all face challenges in
our jobs, with our finances, within our families, and in our
friendships and relationships with others. And, even with
early successes in the war on terrorism, Americans will find
it increasingly difficult to experience peace here at home
now that our country must become a much more fortified
nation, literally, figuratively, and emotionally. With polls
showing almost one-third of the population fearing further
terrorism and almost one-half knowing someone who has
lost a job recently, how can we find contentment and expe-

rience peace in the new America?

Jesus' birth and resurrection are both framed by references to peace. When Jesus was born, the angel who appeared to the shepherds in the fields outside Bethlehem said to them: "'Do not be afraid. I bring you good news of great joy that will be for all the people. Today in the town of David a Savior has been born to you; he is Christ the Lord. This will be a sign to you: You will find a baby wrapped in cloths and lying in a manger.' Suddenly a great company of the heavenly host appeared with the angel, praising God and saying, 'Glory to God in the highest, and on earth peace to men on whom his favor rests'" (Luke 2:10–14). And, when Jesus appeared to His disciples following His resurrection, His first words were "Peace be with you" (Luke 24:36). Thus, the bookends of Jesus' life were marked with a proclamation that His birth would bring peace to those who would follow Him as He lived an earthly life, and to those who would continue to believe in Him after his death and resurrection.

In John 14:27, Jesus asks that we have faith in Him, and through that faith we receive His gift of peace. He also commands us to not let our hearts be troubled or to be afraid. If we live in fear, we fail to trust God and cannot achieve the peace Jesus speaks of in this passage. In these difficult times, and even in less stressful times, we all experience fear. We fear not being accepted by our peers. We fear failure in school, in our work, and/or in our relationships with others. Some may experience a true physical fear of abuse or neglect. By believing in God's omnipotence and His power to overcome evil, we can defeat our fear and enable God's gift of life to mature within our hearts. Peace is the foundation of the "perfect love" that "drives out fear" and enables us to grow in our relationship with God. Faith is the driver. Without faith, our fears overcome us and true peace is unreachable. With faith, we gain the strength that can only come from God's power—a strength and resolve that can overcome fear and hate.

Consider Psalm 29:11: "The Lord gives strength to his people; the Lord blesses his people with peace." The Psalmist draws on God's strength to find true peace.

Peace is also associated with doing good and turning from evil: "Turn from evil and do good; seek peace and pursue it" (Psalm 34:14). We must humble ourselves before God if we are to master true peace. Our self-importance, our selfishness, and our misguided belief that we alone are responsible for our fate and our success must be checked at God's door. Instead, we must humble ourselves before God to inherit the peace He intends for us to enjoy: "A little while, and the wicked will be no more; though you look for them, they will not be found. But the meek will inherit the land and enjoy great peace" (Psalm 37:10, 11).

Thus, the meek—not the powerful or self-righteous—will inherit God's kingdom and enjoy great peace. Consider the people we admire in America today—are they religious or political leaders, social workers, and teachers, or are they media moguls, CEOs, movie stars, and wealthy athletes? Again, the meek, and those who humble themselves, will enjoy peace. We will never find contentment in life if we constantly strive for more and more earthly riches: "A heart at peace gives life to the body, but envy rots the bones" (Proverbs 14:30). Open your heart and mind to God's word, submit and humble yourself before God, and pray for peace. "Submit to God and be at peace with him; in this way prosperity will come to you" (Job 22:21).

Finally, we are to spread God's peace to others. Jesus commanded us to "Go! I am sending you out like lambs among wolves. Do not take a purse or bag or sandals; and do not greet anyone on the road. When you enter a house, first say, 'Peace to this house.' If a man of peace is there, your peace will rest on him; if not, it will return to you" (Luke 10:3–6).

We can spread God's peace through actively applying the fruit of the spirit to our lives. Love, kindness, goodness, faithfulness, and gentleness toward others can spread God's love and joy and bring peace to others. Again, although they are discussed separately in this book, the fruit of the spirit are divinely intertwined, and together they bring us, and those we touch and affect daily, closer to God and His ultimate plan for our lives.

Chapter V.

Patience

.

Be completely humble and gentle; be patient, bearing
with one another in love. Make every effort to keep the
unity of the Spirit through the bond of peace. (Ephesians
4:2, 3)

Peace and patience go hand in hand. As Paul states in
Ephesians above, patient love yields unity with the Holy
Spirit in peace. God instructs us numerous times in the Bible
to be patient. Again, patience in America today is really
unnecessary, which is why patience is so difficult to achieve
personally and so hard to pass on to our children. Why save
for something when credit is readily available, even to high
school and college students who have no source of income?
Credit cards and debt are the American way—ninety days
same as cash! We have the unique opportunity in America to
live, at least for a time, well above our means and to live a
false life. Even on the heels of the most significant economic
boom in our nation's history, the slightest downturn in the
economy triggered a wave of personal and business bankrupt-
cies virtually unprecedented in America. The tech bubble

wiped out billions in market value of our 401(k) plans, and instantly made paupers of millionaires (on paper). Our savings rate is virtually non-existent, and consumers are refinancing their high interest credit cards into home equity lines and loans that tap into their last bastion of net worth—their homes. Why are we so impatient?

The war on terrorism is another example. President Bush, his cabinet members, and our military urged caution and prepared us for a long, tough war with the potential to last years. In spite of this, within weeks of the start of the war effort, our mainstream media reported that the American people thought, "the war isn't going well," "this looks like another Vietnam," and "things appear stalled." As we all know, the Taliban fell in Afghanistan merely weeks after the American war effort began. Consider the patience of the World War II generation—America's first response to the Japanese attack on Pearl Harbor came over four *months* after December 7, 1941. America's military response to September 11, 2001, came a mere four *weeks* later, with resounding successes within two months of the beginning of the campaign.

I trust that President Bush may have been guided by Paul's words in Ecclesiastes 7:8, 9: "The end of a matter is better than its beginning, and patience is better than pride. Do not be quickly provoked in your spirit, for anger resides in the lap of fools." Our anger after September 11th seethed; we wanted immediate retaliation, and justly so. However, our President and military proceeded with patience and caution, rather than with anger and pride. Had we proceeded otherwise, might we have angered the world community rather than building a world coalition against terrorism? Might we have rushed to invade Al Qaeda's caves, only to be ambushed at every turn, costing numerous American lives? Another passage may sum up the performance of our President during these trying times: "A patient man has great understanding, but a quick-tempered man displays folly" (Proverbs 14:29).

We should thank God that He is not so hasty with us. How many second chances does God give us? Think of the patience God has shown you. How long will He wait for you to humble yourself before Him, accept Jesus as your Savior, and overcome your worst vices? We should strive for such patience in our dealings with our spouses, our children, and our friends. "Preach the Word; be prepared in season and out of season; correct, rebuke and encourage—with great patience and careful instruction" (2 Timothy 4:2). Think again of Paul's description of love in 1 Corinthians 13. His first words are "Love is patient." The next time you are prone to criticize your spouse, or scream at your kids, consider your love for them, and whether you are obeying God's command for patience. Remember also the patience with which God judges us. Tread lightly, gently, and with "careful instruction."

Obviously, people irritate and annoy us, and there are times when we must rebuke them firmly. Otherwise, people might take advantage of us. Who hasn't hung up on a telemarketer who called during a family dinner? But, in our dealings with those we love and our neighbors, we should strive for patience. This doesn't mean that we refrain from disciplining our children or honestly discussing our marital problems, whatever they might be, with our spouses. But, it does mean that we should do so in a caring, loving way. God our Father prunes and disciplines us, and many times we need a painful reminder of the ramifications of our continued sin, because He loves us. (See also Chapter VIII, Gentleness.) We do the same with our children, because we love them. But, we are to rebuke and teach out of love, not out of anger: "Therefore, as God's chosen people, holy and dearly loved, clothe yourselves with compassion, kindness, humility, gentleness and patience. Bear with each other and forgive whatever grievances you may have against one another. Forgive as the Lord forgave you" (Colossians 3:12, 13).

Patience, however, does not mean tolerating continued

abuse or sin against you without consequence. A spouse's repeated unfaithfulness should not be tolerated. As John cautioned in 1 John, we all sin, but one who repeatedly sins without repentance and without striving to overcome such sin mocks God's forgiveness. Do not let your patience be used as a sword against you. Again, we are to be patient with one another, but not with continued sin. God does not ask you to be a victim to one who exploits your application of the fruit of the spirit to your own life. Patience goes hand in hand with loving God, seeking to please Him, engaging in good works, and thanking God faithfully and consistently. Patience and peace are granted to those who please God, enabling us to live our lives according to God's plans without getting frustrated, annoyed, and angry as we seek to do God's will. "And we pray this in order that you may live a life worthy of the Lord and may please him in every way: bearing fruit in every good work, growing in the knowledge of God, being strengthened with all power according to his glorious might so that you may have great endurance and patience, and joyfully giving thanks to the Father, who has qualified you to share in the inheritance of the saints in the kingdom of light" (Colossians 1:10–12).

Finally, it is apparent from various scriptures that early Christians were readying themselves for Christ's return, rather than living and working for the Lord. James sought to rebuke those who would focus too intently on Christ's return at the expense of their worldly responsibilities. His parable of the farmer and the rain cautions us that good things (a valuable crop) come to those who wait, and assures us that Christ will return in His time. We must be ready, but not dwell on the timing of Christ's return: "Be patient, then, brothers, until the Lord's coming. See how the farmer waits for the land to yield its valuable crop and how patient he is for the autumn and spring rains. You too, be patient and stand firm, because the Lord's coming is near" (James 5:7, 8).

Consider also Peter's warning to be ready for the coming of the Lord, but also his advice that to God one day is like a thousand years. He reiterates that Jesus will return in His time, not ours. In the meantime, he urges us to be at peace with God and not to worry of such things:

> But do not forget this one thing, dear friends: With the Lord a day is like a thousand years, and a thousand years are like a day. The Lord is not slow in keeping his promise, as some understand slowness. He is patient with you, not wanting anyone to perish, but everyone to come to repentance. But the day of the Lord will come like a thief. The heavens will disappear with a roar; the elements will be destroyed by fire, and the earth and everything in it will be laid bare. Since everything will be destroyed in this way, what kind of people ought you to be? You ought to live holy and godly lives as you look forward to the day of God and speed its coming. That day will bring about the destruction of the heavens by fire, and the elements will melt in the heat. But in keeping with his promise we are looking forward to a new heaven and a new earth, the home of righteousness. So then, dear friends, since you are looking forward to this, make every effort to be found spotless, blameless and at peace with him. Bear in mind that our Lord's patience means salvation, just as our dear brother Paul also wrote you with the wisdom that God gave him. (2 Peter 3:8–15)

Our reward of eternal life will arrive, whether by our earthly death or by way of Jesus' coming. The timing of our meeting with Jesus should not be of concern. Our focus should instead be on the substance of that meeting. Note also the mention again of God's patience with us. He wants to give us ample time to repent and to accept Jesus Christ as our savior. God does not want us to perish; instead, He wants us to come, through our free choice, to Him in our time. Likewise, in seeking to emulate Christ, we should incorporate and pray for a sense of peace and patience in our relationships—both with those we love and with God.

Chapter VI.

Kindness and Goodness

Get rid of all bitterness, rage and anger, brawling and slander, along with every form of malice. Be kind and compassionate to one another, forgiving each other, just as in Christ God forgave you. (Ephesians 4:31, 32)

For it is by grace you have been saved, through faith— and this not from yourselves, it is the gift of God—not by works, so that no one can boast. For we are God's workmanship, created in Christ Jesus to do good works, which God prepared in advance for us to do. (Ephesians 2:8–10)

Love is patient, love is kind. True love surely is. God exhibited His great love for us, and the ultimate kindness, in sacrificing his own perfect Son for us. "And God raised us up with Christ and seated us with him in the heavenly realms in Christ Jesus, in order that in the coming ages he might show the incomparable riches of his grace, expressed in his kindness to us in Christ Jesus. For it is by grace you have been saved, through faith—and this not from yourselves, it is the gift of God" (Ephesians 2:6–8). Such kindness is a gift from God, and it is God's grace that also calls us to extend such grace and kindness to others. Scripture is clear that our good works and good deeds do not save us, but instead we are saved by God's grace. Just as He has forgiven us, we are to forgive others: "Forgive us our debts, as we also have forgiven our debtors."

However, our faith is "dead" without action—good deeds. Our words pale in comparison to our acts and our works: "What good is it, my brothers, if a man claims to have faith but has no deeds? Can such faith save him? Suppose a brother or sister is without clothes and daily food. If one of you says to him, 'Go, I wish you well; keep warm and well fed,' but does nothing about his physical needs, what good is it? In the same way, faith by itself, if it is not accompanied by action, is dead. But someone will say, 'You have faith; I have deeds.' Show me your faith without deeds, and I will show you my faith by what I do" (James 2:14–18).

Thus, our faith lives through our actions more than through our thoughts or our words. Writing this book has been as convicting for me as it likely is for you to read it. Putting the fruit of the spirit into action in our lives is not easy. It can be frustrating, especially if we feel unappreciated by others, we fail to ourselves heed God's word, or we feel that we are doing "all the work." However, that is why the divine balance of all fruit of the spirit is key. For example, when others we attempt to love reject us, we must pray for patience and peace, and seek to control our emotions.

We cannot change others, including our spouse or our kids, by demanding that they change. We can profoundly work only on ourselves, and change our own attitudes, desires, and focus. Only then will others possibly change through our expressions of the fruit of the spirit. Pray that God's kindness and goodness will literally transform your life. Consider the phenomenal effects of God's kindness in Titus 3:3–5: "At one time we too were foolish, disobedient, deceived and enslaved by all kinds of passions and pleasures. We lived in malice and envy, being hated and hating one another. But when the kindness and love of God our Savior appeared, he saved us, not because of righteous things we had done, but because of his mercy. He saved us through the washing of rebirth and renewal by the Holy Spirit."

Paul speaks of living disobediently and foolishly, giving into every lustful and sensual desire. However, this "freedom" leads to being enslaved by immediate gratification. Instead of wilting before every temptation and desire, Paul asks us to focus on Christ's kindness and love, and on renewing our spirit through God's gift of mercy and kindness. The Holy Spirit renews us through God's kindness and His goodness.

Likewise, in 2 Timothy, Paul asks us to call out to the Lord with a pure heart, free from evil desires and selfishness: "Flee the evil desires of youth, and pursue righteousness, faith, love and peace, along with those who call on the Lord out of a pure heart. Don't have anything to do with foolish and stupid arguments, because you know they produce quarrels. And the Lord's servant must not quarrel; instead, he must be kind to everyone, able to teach, not resentful" (2 Timothy 2:22–24). He asks us not to gossip or to engage in endless "foolish and stupid arguments." Instead, be kind to everyone.

I believe this starts at home. We can be condescending and overly critical of our spouse and our kids. We may say hurtful things we would never say to people we have never even met. But, with the ones we profess to love the most, many times our kindness gets checked at the front doors of our homes. Everyone has bad days. We all struggle with life pressures. For example, barging into the family unit around dinnertime can be like throwing gasoline on a fire, depending upon how we react to such pressures. The kids are screaming; the stay-at-home mom, or the first spouse to return home if both work, is already knee deep in the stress of preparing the family meal, changing diapers, or reviewing the day's school projects or homework. We may resent the fact that no one seems to care we've come home. Our reaction to such a situation may sow the seeds of a whole evening (or more) of quarrels and fights.

Paul asks us to "pursue righteousness, faith, love and peace . . . out of a pure heart" (2 Timothy 2:22). If you have trouble making the work-to-home transition in a peaceful, loving way, pray on the way home. Turn off the garden report or the nightly sports radio program and sincerely pray for God's guidance and for His peace. Or, listen to Christian, jazz, or classical music on the way home. Use the drive home as a transition from the wars of the day to peaceful nights. Your family will appreciate your gift of kindness and will be at peace. When was the last time you brought flowers home to your spouse out of the blue? When was the last time you wrote a quick little love note and placed it in your spouse's briefcase or purse, or your child's lunchbox? When was the last time you willingly took on and completed your spouse's typical chore without being asked? Shower your kindness on others, and you will receive kindness in return. What goes around comes around, particularly within our families. We reap what we sow.

We are also commanded to be kind to those in need: "He who despises his neighbor sins, but blessed is he who is kind to the needy" (Proverbs 14:21). Kindness to others is an outward expression of Christ's presence within our hearts. Christ challenged us to treat all people that we encounter with the kindness and love with which we would treat Jesus if He stood before us today. What an awesome responsibility! I doubt any of us greet those we meet in such a profoundly loving manner. Jesus asks us specifically to care for the oppressed, to feed the hungry and to care for strangers:

Then the King will say to those on his right, "Come, you who are blessed by my Father; take your inheritance, the kingdom prepared for you since the creation of the world. For I was hungry and you gave me something to eat, I was thirsty and you gave me something to drink, I was a stranger and you invited me in, I needed clothes and you clothed me, I was sick and you looked after me, I was in prison and you came to visit me."

Then the righteous will answer him, "Lord, when did we see you hungry and feed you, or thirsty and give you something to drink? When did we see you a stranger and invite you in, or needing clothes and clothe you? When did we see you sick or in prison and go to visit you?"

The King will reply, "I tell you the truth, *whatever you did for one of the least of these brothers of mine, you did for me*." (Matthew 25:34–40, italics added)

How often are we labeled a Good Samaritan? How often do we volunteer our talents, our time, and our money to a friend in need, our charities of choice or to our churches? Jesus clearly and concisely commands us to do these things for the least of our brothers. Although pockets of such charity and volunteerism are in America today, we can do so much more. God rewards faithfulness to His word. God knows who serves and who is served, who only gives and who only receives. The least among us can serve others. How well do our actions align with our words?

Consider the extraordinary effort and time given by our public servants at Ground Zero in Manhattan following September 11, 2001. Consider those who stood in line to donate blood. Consider the ones who contributed their treasures to the over $1 billion in aid raised for the victims of the terrorist attacks on America. I hope you can count yourself among those who gave of the vast resources and riches to which God has entrusted you. But giving of ourselves and our resources during one month of our lives, and in response to such a great and obvious need, is not God's call. He expects so much more. We are to live to give.

And when we do give, we should give for the right reasons. Do you give so that you can get a new church wing named after you? Do you give so that your name appears in a charity mailing so that you can boast to others of your giving? Consider Jesus' words about giving: "But when you give to the needy, do not let your left hand know what your right hand is doing, so that your giving may be in secret. *Then your Father, who sees what is done in secret, will reward you*" (Matthew 6:3, 4, italics added). Give to your church and to your favorite charities out of love and kindness, not out of an expectation for a return gift, recognition, or God's blessings, or out of pride. God has already given us the gift of eternal life, if we will receive it openly. No other earthly gift—whether gratitude on the part of those who are helped by our giving, or our own pride—can compare to God's great gift for us, which should be enough.

Consider Paul's words to Timothy: "Command those who are rich in this present world not to be arrogant nor to put their hope in wealth, which is so uncertain, but to put their hope in God, who richly provides us with everything for our enjoyment. Command them to do good, to be rich in good deeds, and to be generous and willing to share. In this way they will lay up treasure for themselves as a firm foundation for the coming age, so that they may take hold of the life that is truly life (1 Timothy 6:17–19).This passage nicely brings together Paul's commands (a) not to love money or place our hopes in wealth; (b) to humbly realize that all of our talents are God-given (see Chapter II on Selfish Love); and (c) to turn from arrogance, greed, and envy, and instead "be generous and willing to share" our riches with others.

Paul's commands are so convicting, especially in our prosperous society. We all are conditioned to look the other way when people are truly in need. We believe the American Dream is there for the taking for all those who work hard, and if we reach it, it is because of "me," and if we fail to reach it, it is our own fault. However, so many things make up a person's lot in life—education, opportunity, parental influences, peers, and, of course, hard work. Therefore, we must be careful not to judge others' circumstances, since we have not walked in their shoes.

However, the scripture is also clear in that God does not reward laziness, and God does not command us to reward laziness with handouts to those who are able-bodied and can work, but choose not to do so. The Bible is chock full of cautions regarding laziness. "Lazy hands make a man poor, but diligent hands bring wealth. He who gathers crops in summer is a wise son, but he who sleeps during harvest is a disgraceful son" (Proverbs 10:4, 5). "If a man is lazy, the rafters sag; if his hands are idle, the house leaks" (Ecclesiastes 10:18).

Consider also Paul's description of laziness in 2 Thessalonians 3:8–10. Paul is describing how he and his friends worked hard, earned their keep, and paid for their food while ministering in Thessalonica. Paul is not condemning rest and relaxation, but true slothfulness: "We worked night and day, laboring and toiling so that we would not be a burden to any of you. We did this, not because we do not have the right to such help, but in order to make ourselves a model for you to follow. For even when we were with you, we gave you this rule: *'If a man will not work, he shall not eat'*" (italics added). Paul instead condemns the busybodies who have chosen to cease work and prepare for the coming of the Lord. Paul calls them to end such idleness and gossip and "never tire of doing what is right" (2 Thessalonians 3:13). Paul even advised the church to stop associating with those who would not work, so that shame would drive these able-bodied people back to work. Paul does not advocate cruelty, but instead calls the church to lovingly prune and discipline those who abdicate their responsibilities. In the context of our charity to others, we must be on guard for the lazy among us who will try to exploit our cheerful giving for their own gains.

Jesus, in the parable of the industrious and lazy managers, also cautions us not to waste our God-given talents and the money and property to which we have been entrusted, but instead to use our talents to grow what God has entrusted to us:

> Again, it will be like a man going on a journey, who called his servants and entrusted his property to them. To one he gave five talents of money, to another two talents, and to another one talent, each according to his ability. Then he went on his journey. The man who had received the five talents went at once and put his money to work and gained five more. So also, the one with the two talents gained two more. But the man who had received the one talent went off, dug a hole in the ground and hid his master's money.

> After a long time the master of those servants returned and settled accounts with them. The man who had received the five talents brought the other five. "Master," he said, "you entrusted me with five talents. See, I have gained five more." His master replied, "Well done, good and faithful servant! You have been faithful with a few things; I will put you in charge of many things. Come and share your master's happiness!"

The man with the two talents also came. "Master," he said, "you entrusted me with two talents; see, I have gained two more." His master replied, "Well done, good and faithful servant! You have been faithful with a few things; I will put you in charge of many things. Come and share your master's happiness!"

Then the man who had received the one talent came. "Master," he said, "I knew that you are a hard man, harvesting where you have not sown and gathering where you have not scattered seed. So I was afraid and went out and hid your talent in the ground. See, here is what belongs to you." His master replied, "You wicked, lazy servant! So you knew that I harvest where I have not sown and gather where I have not scattered seed?" (Matthew 25:14–26)

The master in Jesus' parable punishes the "wicked and lazy servant." Therefore, although we are to give freely of our time, our talents, and our money to others, we must act prudently and as good stewards in doing so. We should carefully examine any charities we contribute to outside of our church to ensure that our gifts are used for the right reasons and for those who are truly in need. Again, we must be careful of making rash judgments of others' situations. Instead, we must trust our church and the charities to which we donate our time, talents, and treasure to allocate such gifts responsibly.

How do we serve others as God would have us serve? Jesus is the greatest example of one who deserved only to be served, yet He served others. Jesus served even in His last hours just before his "last supper," even when He knew that one of his disciples had betrayed Him. Was He angry? Was He accusatory in tone? No, instead, He served:

Jesus knew that the Father had put all things under his power, and that he had come from God and was returning to God; so he got up from the meal, took off his outer clothing, and wrapped a towel around his waist. After that, he poured water into a basin and began to wash his disciples' feet, drying them with the towel that was wrapped around him.

He came to Simon Peter, who said to him, "Lord, are you going to wash my feet?" Jesus replied, "You do not realize now what I am doing, but later you will understand." "No," said Peter, "you shall never wash my feet." Jesus answered, "Unless I wash you, you have no part with me. . . ."

When he had finished washing their feet, he put on his clothes and returned to his place. "Do you understand what I have done for you?" he asked them. "You call me 'Teacher' and 'Lord,' and rightly so, for that is what I am. Now that I, your Lord and Teacher, have washed your feet, you also should wash one another's feet. *I have set you an example that you should do as I have done for you. I tell you the truth, no servant is greater than his master*, nor is a messenger greater than the one who sent him. Now that you know these things, you will be blessed if you do them. (John 13:3–17, italics added)

Jesus picked a servant's job to provide an unforgettable last example of service to his disciples. Washing guests' feet was a common chore for a household servant in Biblical times. Jesus' telling example of service is that if the Son of God is no more mighty than a servant, and serves others with such humbleness, how much more must we serve to gain God's approval? Jesus knew that by exemplifying service to his disciples, that they would in turn exemplify service to all those to whom they were to preach His gospel. What a lasting picture!

How often do we openly exhibit the kindness Jesus displayed to His disciples and others? Jesus asked that our first priority be to love the Lord God with all of our hearts. Secondly, He asked us to love our neighbors as ourselves. Only when we challenge our own worldly priorities and realign them according to God's plan will we find true joy and happiness in life: "As God's chosen people, holy and dearly loved, clothe yourselves with compassion, kindness, humility, gentleness and patience. Bear with each other and forgive whatever grievances you may have against one another. Forgive as the Lord forgave you" (Colossians 3:12, 13). We must step up to God's challenge. Only through applying the fruit of the spirit to our lives will we one day hear our Lord God say, "Well done, good and faithful servant!" (Matthew 25:23).

Chapter VII.

Faithfulness

And pray that we may be delivered from wicked and evil men, for not everyone has faith. But the Lord is faithful, and he will strengthen and protect you from the evil one. We have confidence in the Lord that you are doing and will continue to do the things we command. (2 Thessalonians 3:2–4)

If the Lord is so faithful, as Paul claims in 2 Thessalonians 3:3, why did He not protect the victims of the September 11, 2001, terrorist attacks "from the evil one"? The first questions on many lips on the morning of September 11, 2001, were "Where was God?" and "If God is a loving, compassionate God, how can He permit such tragedy?" Bob Russell, senior pastor of Southeast Christian Church in Louisville, Kentucky, answered these questions by stating that God is sovereign, but He respects us so much that He gives us freedom. This freedom to love, or to hate, is discussed in greater detail in Chapter II, but I believe Pastor Russell's examples of such freedom, and implicitly the potential costs of granting us such freedom, speak volumes on this issue:

Where was God last Tuesday? The same place you parents are when your 16-year-old gets in the car and drives off and you say, "Oh, I hope he listens to what I said."

Where was God last Tuesday? The same place the father of the prodigal son was when his son was hurting in the far country: standing on the front porch, watching and hoping he would come back.

Where was God last Tuesday? The same place He was when His Son was dying on the cross and people were gloating over His death—waiting in the shadows, knowing there would be victory and resurrection.

God gives us great freedom, and our choices in the face of such freedom determine our destiny. Even when faced with great trials, we must remain faithful, and we must draw upon our faith to lead us through such strife. As mentioned in Chapter III, "Peace," many times we cannot achieve the true peace God offers us without facing great troubles and pruning in our lives. Also, many times we cannot grow as men or women, or as Christians, without experiencing the pain and regret that our choices cause to ourselves and to others. Would Charles Colson have started his great prison ministry if he had not served time in prison himself? Would I be writing this book if I had not experienced the hollow "happiness" of status and money at the expense of my family and faith? Sometimes we realize what is truly important to us, or realize that there are consequences to our free choices, only when our choices cause pain. During difficult times, we can make the best of our opportunities and humble ourselves before God, or else we can turn away from God in disbelief.

Pastor Russell also talked about an interview with people who had lived through World War II in London. When asked what their favorite time of their lives was, nearly all of them responded "World War II," even though London was bombed almost daily during the war. When asked why, the almost universal response was "Well, you know when you live under the threat of death, every day is precious." I do not believe God causes tragedies to happen. They instead happen largely as a result of freedom gone awry. Instead, our reaction to such heartache, pain, and evil—as in the case of the terrorist attacks—will either draw us closer to God or drive a wedge between God and us. So far, many in America seem to be making the wise choice. Let's hope it continues.

Even when we question our faith, God remains faithful. His promise of eternal life through His son Jesus Christ is the rock upon which the world's salvation has been and will be based until Jesus returns. Consider Romans 3:3, 4: "What if some did not have faith? Will their lack of faith nullify God's faithfulness? Not at all! Let God be true, and every man a liar." God's word remains true, regardless of men's faith, or lack thereof. Those who continue to reject faith live a lie; those who eventually come to Christ can depend on God's faithfulness, knowing that, until Christ's return, anyone can come to Christ and count on His everlasting love and salvation.

Faithfulness also means that we should remain faithful to God's commandments and obey His word. Thus, Christians must read and study the word of God, adhere to the commandments, apply the fruit of the spirit to their lives, and strive to be "good and faithful servants" to God: "So then, men ought to regard us as servants of Christ and as those entrusted with the secret things of God. Now it is required that those who have been given a trust must prove faithful" (1 Corinthians 4:1, 2).

As Paul states in 1 Corinthians, Christians have been given a great gift of eternal life. To remain in God's favor, as trustees of God's message of love and hope, we must prove ourselves faithful to Him in all we do. As we practice our faith and prove faithful, God grants us peace. "To the saints in Ephesus, the faithful in Christ Jesus: Grace and peace to you from God our Father and the Lord Jesus Christ" (Ephesians 1:1, 2). As discussed in Chapter II, "Love," God is faithful in His promise to forgive us of our sins, if in fact we honestly and sincerely confess our sins and pledge to turn from our corrupt ways. Such confession frees us to grow in our fellowship with God, and should ease our minds. God is forever faithful and just in his promise to forgive us, even when we fail again and again. His forgiveness is a gift: "If we claim to be without sin, we deceive ourselves and the truth is not in us. If we confess our sins, he is faithful and just and will forgive us our sins and purify us from all unrighteousness. If we claim we have not sinned, we make him out to be a liar and his word has no place in our lives" (1 John 1:8–10).

Accept God's purification from unrighteousness, and do not dwell on your failures. However, do not test God's faithfulness. True confession involves a commitment to not continue or repeat our sins. Are we really asking for temporary forgiveness when we pray to God? Do we mentally wink at God when we confess, knowing that we will continue to engage in that same sin again and again? If so, we desecrate God's great gift of forgiveness and eternal life.

When faced with temptation, pray to God for strength. As Christians, we must call upon our personal relationship with Jesus to strengthen our resolve in the face of temptations: "He will keep you strong to the end, so that you will be blameless on the day of our Lord Jesus Christ. God, who has called you into fellowship with his Son Jesus Christ our Lord, is faithful" (1 Corinthians 1:8, 9).Again, God is reliable and dependable, and will grant us the strength we need to overcome sin. "God is faithful; he will not let you be tempted beyond what you can bear. But when you are tempted, he will also provide a way out so that you can stand up under it" (1 Corinthians 10:13).

We are continually bombarded with temptations, especially within an American society in which greed, envy, pornography, divorce, adultery, teen sex, and explicit music and videos are so prevalent and so widely accepted. Such temptations are only the tip of the iceberg in the freewheeling and carefree civilization in which we now live. I submit that we Americans face sinful temptations that no other society in the earth's history has faced, and now more than ever, we must rely on God's faithfulness to help us fight such easy-to-follow paths to sin. For example, at your fingertips via the internet, you can view criminally explicit sexual images, and/or foolishly gamble away your life savings to online sports books and online poker tables. And, with more and more women in the workplace, women, as well as men, now face temptations that test their faithfulness and fidelity to their families. Pray continually for God's wisdom and strength in the face of your particular sinful leanings.

In terms of our earthly relationships, God first and foremost commands us to remain faithful to our families, and to our spouses in particular: "'I tell you that anyone who divorces his wife, except for marital unfaithfulness, and marries another woman commits adultery.' The disciples said to him, 'If this is the situation between a husband and wife, it is better not to marry.' Jesus replied, 'Not everyone can accept this word, but only those to whom it has been given'" (Matthew 19:9–11).

Jesus' words leave nothing to debate regarding the marriage relationship. He clearly calls us to remain faithful to our spouses, given that God has ordained marriage as sacred. "The man said, 'This is now bone of my bones and flesh of my flesh; she shall be called "woman," for she was taken out of man.' For this reason a man will leave his father and mother and be united to his wife, and they will become one flesh" (Genesis 2:23, 24). When two people marry, they become one flesh. We cannot literally cut off portions of our own bodies that annoy, itch, or hurt us. Instead, we must work to scratch our itches, and cultivate and nurse back to health our injuries or our sicknesses, so that we become whole again.

I have previously discussed the sins and temptations that threaten our relationships with our families, and will do so again in Chapter VIII, "Gentleness," so I will not reiterate the details here. But, I do ask that you deeply consider God's call for you to lift up your marriage to Him, and pray that your marriage comes second only to your relationship with God. Satan would like nothing better than to destroy our marriages, destroy our families, and jeopardize our children, which in turn endangers our entire civilization.

Consider the strong words of Paul in his letter to the Corinthians about the sanctity of marriage. As in America today, such times in Corinth were fraught with sexual immorality and prostitution. Today in America we face the same immorality, including not only legalized prostitution and pornography, but also AIDS, sexually transmitted diseases, and teen pregnancies. Paul's words hit the nail on the head now more than ever before: "But since there is so much immorality, each man should have his own wife, and each woman her own husband. The husband should fulfill his marital duty to his wife, and likewise the wife to her husband. The wife's body does not belong to her alone but also to her husband. In the same way, the husband's body does not belong to him alone but also to his wife. Do not deprive each other except by mutual consent and for a time, so that you may devote yourselves to prayer. Then come together again so that Satan will not tempt you because of your lack of self-control" (1 Corinthians 7:2–5).

Sexual temptations have drawn in even the most righteous of men and women. Such temptations are so difficult to reject since our bodies are programmed to love and to lust. Paul offers up marriage as a way in which we may satisfy our sexual desires with our life partners whom we are to love (not merely lust), just as Jesus loved the church, in God's planned, sacred way. Notice again Paul's call to equality among the sexes. Just as in his beautiful description of "love" in 1 Corinthians, even in Biblical times, Paul preached that a husband's body belongs to his wife, and vice versa. Look back at Matthew 19:10. Even Jesus' own disciples reasoned that it might be best not to marry if a man were to commit adultery by divorcing his wife! But, consider Proverbs 6:25–29: "Do not lust in your heart after her beauty or let her captivate you with her eyes, for the prostitute reduces you to a loaf of bread, and the adulteress preys upon your very life. Can a man scoop fire into his lap without his clothes being burned? Can a man walk on hot coals without his feet being scorched? So is he who sleeps with another man's wife; no one who touches her will go unpunished."

The scripture is clear. What, then, are we to make of all of the divorces in America today? Even fifty percent of Christian marriages end in divorce. I do not have all of the answers, but I do submit that if we each strive to apply the fruit of the spirit to our lives, and to our marriages in particular, divorces would become a relic of the past. Will this happen? Not for everyone, but for those who truly heed God's word, divorce should be unnecessary.

On the other hand, there are clearly justified grounds for divorce. Jesus clearly states in Matthew 19:10 that unfaithfulness in marriage constitutes grounds for divorce. In addition, an abusive or neglectful spouse can exploit our faithfulness. I have been a product of two divorces as a child, and each divorce, unfortunately, was necessary to protect the physical and emotional well-being of the children. I do not think Jesus asks us to submit to such abuse or neglect. As I have discussed many times in this book, we all sin, and God will forgive our sins if we humbly confess and sincerely ask for God's forgiveness. He also commands us to forgive others. However, outside of the grace offered by God, the decision to offer forgiveness for marital infidelity, neglect, or abuse is solely within the purview of the husband, wife, or child who is the victim of such sin. And one may forgive, but not truly forget, and earthly consequences remain, even if we sincerely plead for and receive God's forgiveness.

For example, I have forgiven my father for deserting our family and for failing to support my sister and me emotionally and financially following my parents' divorce. My wife and I have opened our home and our hearts to him, only to be disappointed in his response. I am now at peace due to God's call to forgive him, but without a heartfelt plea on his part for forgiveness, and without a sincere desire by him to change and make amends, he will remain separated from me and from my children.

Another example of the earthly consequences of our misdeeds is then-Governor George W. Bush's refusal to grant a stay of the execution of convicted murderer Carla Faye Tucker in Texas. There was absolutely no doubt about Ms. Tucker's guilt. Her lawyers even admitted that she killed her victims, and she had admitted the murders in interviews. Ms. Tucker and an accomplice (who died in prison in 1993 from liver disease) broke into a man's house to steal motorcycle parts. Tucker killed him and a second victim, who was hiding under a blanket, with a pickax. She was subsequently sentenced to death and her appeals were exhausted.

Ms. Tucker later professed to become a Christian. However, Mr. Bush did not use his position of power to circumvent the judicial process and to alleviate Ms. Tucker's punishment for her crimes, even though he might have believed in her life change. Jim Lehrer of the Public Broadcasting System interviewed Mr. Bush, also a Christian, in April 2000 regarding his decision not to stay Ms. Tucker's execution. Mr. Bush's response:

> While she was on Death Row [she committed her life
> to Christ]. And the reason I knew that was because she
> was on "Larry King Live" and other TV shows telling
> her story, and she was a compelling witness to the Lord,
> I thought. And unfortunately I saw her, and I say unfor-
> tunately because like many other Americans I fell in
> love with her story. And I was most impressed by her,
> and yet my job as the governor of Texas is to uphold the
> law of the land. My job isn't to judge somebody's heart.
> I believe that's up to the almighty God to make that
> decision. And so when confronted with the facts—the
> two questions that a governor—at least I ask—is guilt
> or innocence . . . [she] had full access to the courts of
> law in the state of Texas and Washington, D.C., in the
> federal courts—when I answered those affirmatively, I
> signed the—the execution went forward.

Whether we are for or against capital punishment, the
point is that sometimes we pay a steep price for our actions,
even if we sincerely repent, vow to make amends, and seek
and receive God's forgiveness and faithfulness. Consider
also Luke 23:39–43, which records the only "deathbed"
salvation in the Bible, which took place while Jesus hung on
the cross between two criminals: "One of the criminals who
hung there hurled insults at him: 'Aren't you the Christ?
Save yourself and us!' But the other criminal rebuked him.
'Don't you fear God,' he said, 'since you are under the same
sentence? We are punished justly, for we are getting what
our deeds deserve. But this man has done nothing wrong.'
Then he said, 'Jesus, remember me when you come into
your kingdom.' Jesus answered him, 'I tell you the truth,
today you will be with me in paradise.'"

Note that Christ did not pardon the repentant thief of his

earthly crimes and then remove him from his cross. The thief was still held accountable for his crimes in this life even though he had made amends with Jesus to be prepared for the next one. Similarly, in the case of Ms. Tucker, Mr. Bush rightly deferred judgment to God as to whether Ms. Tucker's conversion to Christ was genuine.

Sometimes our road to God's forgiveness is littered with earthly debts that must be satisfied. Although we can count on God to be faithful, we must also right any wrongs that we may have caused to secure forgiveness from our spouse, children, family, and friends. The two go hand in hand. If we sincerely ask God for forgiveness, and He faithfully and lovingly grants it, we in turn will surely, as touched by God's hands and as the Holy Spirit dwells within us, put into action the fruit of the spirit in seeking out those we have wronged. We should sincerely apologize, plead for forgiveness, and make right the wrongs we've caused (if we can). God's forgiveness should be a sobering realization of our own failings, and should spur us to "never tire of doing what is right," including humbling ourselves before those we have hurt.

Finally, the New Testament ends with John's chilling warning that in the end times many of us will be tested, and will be imprisoned by Satan for our faith in Jesus: "Do not be afraid of what you are about to suffer. I tell you, the devil will put some of you in prison to test you, and you will suffer persecution for ten days. Be faithful, even to the point of death, and I will give you the crown of life" (Revelation 2:10).

Jesus, however, promises each of us the "crown of life" if we remain faithful to Him, even in the face of death. This passage sadly reminds me of Cassie Bernall, the young junior at Columbine High School in Littleton, Colorado, who was asked by a gun-toting classmate on April 20, 1999, whether she believed in God. She said, "Yes." In *She Said Yes: The Unlikely Martyrdom of Cassie Bernall*, Cassie's mother, Misty Bernall, describes the terrifying last moments of her daughter's life:

> One student remembers seeing her under a table, hands clasped in prayer; another says she remained seated. Josh, a sophomore who spoke with me a few weeks after the incident, did not see her at all, but he says he will never forget what he heard as he crouched under a desk about twenty-five feet away:
>
> "I couldn't see anything when those guys came up to Cassie, but I could recognize her voice. I could hear everything like it was right next to me. One of them asked her if she believed in God. She paused, like she didn't know what she was going to answer, and *then she said yes. She must have been scared, but her voice didn't sound shaky. It was strong.* Then they asked her why, though they didn't give her a chance to respond. *They just blew her away.*"
>
> Josh says that the way the boys questioned Cassie made him wonder whether she was visibly praying. [italics added]

How would you respond to such a question if faced with certain death? Would you remain faithful to Christ and inherit the "crown of life," as did Cassie Bernall? Would I? I hope and pray that neither we nor our loved ones ever have to step into her shoes in our lifetime, but I pray that if we do, we remain faithful to God. I fearfully pray for the courage of Cassie Bernall and pray for God's peace.

Our faithfulness is tested every day in circumstances much less momentous than the life-or-death test of Cassie Bernall. She passed the ultimate test with flying colors, while many times we fail our own mid-level exams every day. If you are a businessman, when you are away on business, do you accompany your colleagues to strip bars? Do you order pornographic movies through your hotel television? Even worse, do you physically cheat on your spouse? If you're in a college fraternity, do you take advantage of coeds who have had too much to drink? If you have failed to make the girls' soccer team, get a key role in the school play, or get accepted into your favorite college, have you resorted to gossip to tear down those who did? Do you regularly miss dinner with your family or your child's nighttime prayers on account of work? Do you gamble away your children's college funds at the track, the casinos, or on the lottery? How do you respond to temptation? Do you remain faithful—to God, to your spouse, to your children, and to your friends? *Our* faithfulness to God, our families, and our friends is in our own hands—the choice is ours alone. *God's* faithfulness does not waver.

Chapter VIII.

Gentleness

A gentle answer turns away wrath, but a harsh word stirs up anger. The tongue of the wise commends knowledge, but the mouth of the fool gushes folly. (Proverbs 15:1, 2)

Communication, or the lack thereof, can either save a family or a relationship or destroy one. We get so caught up with running to the next appointment, to the next errand, etc., that we tend to be curt and short-tempered when things do not go according to our plans. How often have you uttered a short word at your spouse, or screamed at your kids, and then immediately regretted sticking your foot in your mouth? To top it off, many times our pride restrains us from righting the situation. Thus, it only gets worse. Terse words are returned, and the day, or the night, is shot. The Bible warns us of the consequences of using harsh, foolish words. Instead, we are to be gentle in word and deed, even with strangers.

Marriage

We are to "pursue" gentleness (1 Timothy 6:11). This is particularly true in the marriage relationship. Would your spouse consider you a gentle partner in marriage, even when stirred to anger? Consider the mistakes we all make in life. How important are many of the things that test our patience and stir us to anger? The fruit of the spirit—particularly love, patience, kindness, and gentleness—call upon us to hold our tongue when our words can sting like daggers. Again, "the tongue of the wise commends knowledge" (Proverbs 15:2). As stated many times in this book, it is tough to isolate our discussion of individual fruit of the spirit, since they are all so divinely intertwined. For example, without love and patience, how gentle would we really be?

Our spouses need and deserve gentle touches. So many things can be said without words. Frequent hugging. Holding hands. Caressing your spouse's shoulder. Enfolding welcoming arms around your spouse. Gentle physical touches are so integral to a marriage. Remember, you are "one flesh"! Thus, treat your spouse as you would treat yourself—with kind words and a gentle hand. On the other hand, under absolutely no circumstances are we to use any form of physical discipline or verbal abuse with our spouses. Consider Peter's clear words to marriage partners, and particularly husbands: "Husbands, in the same way be considerate as you live with your wives, and treat them with respect as the weaker partner and as heirs with you of the gracious gift of life, so that nothing will hinder your prayers. Finally, all of you, live in harmony with one another; be sympathetic, love as brothers, be compassionate and humble" (1 Peter 3:7, 8).

If you are a husband, be considerate and treat your wife with respect. The next time you are about to verbally admonish her for spending too freely at the grocery store, or for failing to balance the checkbook or to meet some inconsequential need of yours, think! If you are a wife, the next time you are on the verge of verbally castigating your husband for leaving the toilet seat up, for failing to pick up his dirty socks, or for forgetting to take out the trash, think! Would you scream these identical words to your spouse in public? Would you shout at your co-workers, your boss, your women's Bible study friends, or your golfing buddies the way you do to your own flesh—your spouse? Peter pleads with "all of us" to live in harmony—sympathetically and compassionately. Thus, don't nag your spouse continually. If you have issues, sit down and discuss them honestly and openly. Each of you must commit to listen with an open and humble heart and mind. If you have a short fuse, pray for peace, patience, and gentleness as you fight your urge to put up your defenses and argue to the death. "As a prisoner for the Lord, then, I urge you to live a life worthy of the calling you have received. Be completely humble and gentle; be patient, bearing with one another in love. Make every effort to keep the unity of the Spirit through the bond of peace" (Ephesians 4:1–3).

There is no doubt that even the strongest marriage faces troubles. However, Paul asks us to bear with each other in love, and sometimes we do just that. We persevere in love, even through the tough times. As stated previously, sometimes God prunes us in ways that, at the time, test our faith and possibly even our faith in, or our faithfulness to, our spouses. We may not always understand why things happen if there is a loving, compassionate God, and we may not always understand our spouses and the mistakes they may make in life. But, we must persevere in love and faithfulness, remaining gentle and humble. Continue to practice the fruit of the spirit even in such times, and God will bless your marriage. Without the fruit of the spirit, harmony in your marriage will be fleeting and your marriage will not reap the "gracious gift of life" that Peter described, nor will you experience the peace that God intends for your marriage.

Peter also asks women (and men) to realize the true beauty of a gentle and quiet spirit, and a beauty that does not fade with time. He calls upon us to see the beauty within us, espe- cially within women, who even in Biblical times appear to have been overly concerned about their looks: "Your beauty should not come from outward adornment, such as braided hair and the wearing of gold jewelry and fine clothes. Instead, it should be that of your inner self, the unfading beauty of a gentle and quiet spirit, which is of great worth in God's sight. For this is the way the holy women of the past who put their hope in God used to make themselves beauti- ful" (1 Peter 3:3–5).

Even two thousand years ago, Peter knew that women faced such pressures to measure up to men's and their own standards. Imagine what Peter would say in America today, as women are pressured into bulimia and anorexia in pursuit of *Cosmo* cover good looks and hard bodies. Is there a fashion magazine on the grocery rack without the word "diet" on the cover? What percentage of these magazines are essentially ads for clothes, makeup, diet fixes, etc.? How often is spiritual peace mentioned in *Cosmo*, *GQ*, or *Vogue*, or true love versus simply sexual satisfaction? When women (or some men) seek to emulate the airbrushed models adorning the pages of these magazines, they set themselves up for disappointment. Such a pursuit is akin to the never-ending quest for money and power that many in the business world face. Peter invites us all to realize the pure beauty of those who put their hope in God, not in fashion magazines, the latest fashion, or fading good looks. Again, our culture is exactly the opposite. Ignoring such temptation, when it is rarely out of sight (on TV and the internet, in magazines, newspapers, and movies), is easier said than done.

And if you are a husband, please help in the fight against this culture that seeks to destroy your wife's self-esteem by holding out the carrot of false happiness and joy to those who strive for the unreachable looks promised by our media. Men obviously are drawn to physically attractive women, but it is unfair to hold your spouse up to the manufactured young women you see in magazines, on TV, or in movies. For example, even so-called "soft" pornography in movies, in magazines, or on the internet, in addition to providing an easy avenue to cheat on your wife and violate your bond of faithfulness to her, destroys her self-confidence and her good-hearted desire to look the best she can for you. If she thinks you're never going to be satisfied unless she looks like a centerfold, she has little incentive to try to meet your unrealistic expectations for her. Even most of these beautiful models, as we see them, can't even match up to their *own* fictional personas without plastic surgery, airbrushing, mounds of makeup, and favorable lighting! Both husbands and wives should heed Jesus' words in Matthew: "You have heard that it was said, 'Do not commit adultery.' But I tell you that anyone who looks at a woman lustfully has already committed adultery with her in his heart. If your right eye causes you to sin, gouge it out and throw it away. It is better for you to lose one part of your body than for your whole body to be thrown into hell" (Matthew 5:27–29).

Obviously, Jesus' command on this point is abrupt, but I believe He is driving the point home. Do not lust after another, since you are violating your bond of faithfulness to your spouse by doing so. What is "lust"? We are human, and our eyes are typically drawn toward physical beauty. However, appreciating someone's beauty is one thing; driving around the block for another look is quite another. Realize that your spouse *wants* to look good for you, and to lust after another simply drives a wedge between you and your spouse that may never be removed. He or she wants to trust you, and wants the harmony and peace in marriage that comes from a full marriage, including friendship, love, and a fulfilling sexual relationship.

However, although outward adornment should not be our primary focus, we are also each called to submit to one another in love, and part of that love is displayed by a sincere desire by each of you to appear attractive to each other. "Honor God with your body" by properly caring for yourself: "Do you not know that your body is a temple of the Holy Spirit, who is in you, whom you have received from God? You are not your own; you were bought at a price. Therefore honor God with your body" (1 Corinthians 6 19, 20).

As Christians, our bodies are not our own, since we were bought at a price, and the price was Jesus' death on the cross. Paul commands us to honor God with our bodies by not engaging in sexual immorality, abuse of alcohol or drugs, or a sedentary lifestyle. Although true beauty is found within, we are still to care for ourselves and for our bodies—they are temples of the Holy Spirit—and strive to please our spouses: "For physical training is of some value, but godliness has value for all things, holding promise for both the present life and the life to come" (1 Timothy 4:8). Therefore, please care for yourself, and do not fail to maintain your "temple" for yourself, for your spouse, and for the Lord, who purchased your body. Look first for your spouse's inner beauty, and encourage and compliment his or her inner self as well as outward appearance.

Don't we all know older women, whether widowed or happily married, who just glow with joy? My own grandmother is such a woman. She is eighty-two, and has just in the last few years lost the ability to walk on her own. Every time we bring our kids to see her and my grandfather, she is a little slower in word and movement. But, my how she shines with God's love! What a beauty she is, unconcerned with outer adornment, her gentle, loving, and kind spirit exudes joy. Much of that joy is also due to her loving and patient spouse, my grandfather, a cook in the Army who started his own grocery store and later two restaurants in his small hometown in Kentucky. He is a man of great respect in his church and community. However, I have never heard my grandfather utter a disrespectful word in my grandmother's presence, or to anyone for that matter. He is there pushing her wheelchair with a gentle hand, guiding her into her easy chair, or bringing her a glass of water. He has always approached his marriage, and his children and grandchildren, with a gentle demeanor. My grandparents are devout Christians, and have been a convicting influence on me, not so much by their words, but by their deeds and actions, toward each other and toward our family. They truly have incorporated the fruit of the spirit into their lives. Although their freedom of movement is now restricted, and they cannot enjoy as many Sunday drives and dinners out as they used to, their love for each other and for Christ is a glowing example of the beauty and joy within that Peter so eloquently speaks of in 1 Peter.

Children

God has entrusted us with phenomenal gifts, true miracles, in our children. Likewise, we are to be gentle with them. "Fathers, do not exasperate your children; instead, bring them up in the training and instruction of the Lord" (Ephesians 6:4). As most of us know, children can be a blessing, and they can be, well, a chore. I'm sure you have smiled at the sweet, gentle voice of your two-year-old as she said "milk please," heartened by her show of manners at such a young age, and then you screamed "no" at her thirty seconds later as she flung her sippee cup off her big brother's head. We tend to get exasperated with our children quickly, especially with all that goes on in our busy lives.

When I worked at a large law firm, many times I wouldn't get home until 8:00 or later. My wife insisted that we eat as a family, and I agreed with her then (and agree even more now), except that (at that time), our eighteen-month-old and four-year-old were in meltdown stage by the time I arrived. They were hungry, tired, and ready for bed, and in strolled Daddy. My wife was typically at her wit's end, especially with the eighteen-month-old, who was usually wrapped around one of her legs like a blanket around a piggy. The situation was tense, to say the least. Only after I left the firm, in exchange for a cut in pay and more reasonable hours, did I realize how much happened between 6:00 and 8:00 P.M. every night. My wife was under tremendous pressure to keep a household running, fix dinner, etc., and she'd had the kids for fifteen hours by herself.

We can each help to keep our spouses from losing patience and testing their commitment to gentle discipline and correction when dealing with our children. We do this by taking on greater responsibility around the house, making a firm time commitment to our families, and incorporating the fruit of the spirit into even difficult and frustrating situations. Annoying and frustrating things happen in life, but it is our reactions to these events that define our attitudes and our character.

With respect to our children, we must also pray for peace and patience, and practice the fruit of the spirit in our daily dealings with them. However, we are also called to discipline our children and teach them right from wrong. There is a reason my daughter's kindergarten class scripture for the entire year is Galatians 5:22, 23, the fruit of the spirit. Studying and applying the fruit of the spirit at a young age is integral to our kids' development as young Christians and young citizens. Remember, "train a child in the way he should go, and when he is old he will not turn from it" (Proverbs 22:6).

Hundreds of secular and Christian books have been written on child rearing, but I submit that none is better than the Bible. Note Paul's second letter to Timothy: "All Scripture is God-breathed and is useful for teaching, rebuking, correcting and training in righteousness, so that the man of God may be thoroughly equipped for every good work" (2 Timothy 3:16, 17). What better "life's instruction book" is there than God's own word? We parents are charged with a phenomenal responsibility, and we are called numerous times in the Bible to live up to our responsibilities to our families and our children. Review again the chapters on Love and Faithfulness, and consider again 1 Timothy 5:8: "If anyone does not provide for his relatives, and especially for his immediate family, he has denied the faith and is worse than an unbeliever."

God calls for us not only to financially provide for our families, but also to emotionally care for our children in a gentle and loving way, even in discipline. Obviously, there may be times when discipline must be more than merely taking away privileges or putting your child in "time out." "He who spares the rod hates his son, but he who loves him is careful to discipline him" (Proverbs 13:24). We "hate" our children if we do not properly discipline them, since they obviously do not know what is best for them. A parent's first responsibility is not to be a friend to his or her children, but to teach them, rebuke them, and instruct them in life's lessons. Notice that we should be "careful to discipline" out of "love," not anger. Our discipline must be meted out carefully and must be measured, but also must be done in all seriousness and with an unwavering hand. However, a hug and a kiss should follow so that our kids know that we discipline out of love (i.e., for their own good), just as God's discipline is meted out. We discipline, and then we forgive, just as God many times disciplines and then offers His children forgiveness.

For example, my grandfather apparently was very strict on his three daughters, and did not spare the rod when disciplining them. However, he rarely yelled or screamed. He was gentle in word and doled out his form of discipline in a measured, just, and loving way. All parents, and not just mothers, should take note of Paul's words in 1 Thessalonians 2:6, 7: "As apostles of Christ we could have been a burden to you, but we were gentle among you, like a mother caring for her little children."

Paul's example *assumes* that mothers (and fathers as well) gently care for their children. Unfortunately, many children today are not products of loving and caring parents. Contrast my mother with my father. When I was a child our house became a peaceful refuge only when my father was away. On the other hand, I remember that my loving, gentle, and caring mother was the beacon of my life. I always strived for her approval. I wanted to make her proud.

My father's verbal abuse, directed primarily toward my mother, is a constant reminder to me of how our voices, and particularly men's voices, can frighten children. Parents, before you instinctively scream or yell at your kids, especially young kids, first consider your sheer size in relation to your little ones, and couple that with your authoritative roar. Try to think back to your childhood, whether in a loving home or in a home similar to mine. How did you react to your parents when they became angry? Please pray that God will give you wisdom, gentleness, and patience in dealing with your children.

Children also must commit to obeying their parents. They should be taught God's word about their responsibilities as children and God's commandment that they honor their fathers and mothers: "Listen, my son, to your father's instruction and do not forsake your mother's teaching. They will be a garland to grace your head and a chain to adorn your neck" (Proverbs 1:8, 9).

Our children many times do not understand why they are told "no." They usually do not realize that our instruction and correction is for their own good. I doubt the words in

Proverbs 1 above will change that perception, but it should give us, as parents, hope and comfort that we please God by raising children as we've been instructed by God. Such teaching and discipline, while many times painful for all involved, are necessary and just to raise our kids to follow Christ and to become solid citizens. We can all hope our children will someday say to us, "Mom/Dad, your discipline and teaching really was a garland gracing my head and a beautiful chain adorning my neck!" Don't hold your breath, but I have seen many college kids return to the nest to thank their parents for their wonderful teaching, love, and support over the years.

As we are called to gently love our spouses and raise our children, don't forget to look in the mirror. As stated before, everyone hates a hypocrite, and your children will heed your actions more than your words. Obviously, adults can partake of and do some things that children should not, so you cannot hold yourself to the exact standards to which you hold your children. But generally consider your own life and actions before meting out your discipline. Be wary of self-righteousness in light of your own faults and mistakes. Paul spoke of just this risk in his first letter to Timothy: "If anyone sets his heart on being an overseer, he desires a noble task. Now the overseer must be above reproach, the husband of but one wife, temperate, self-controlled, respectable, hospitable, able to teach, not given to drunkenness, not violent but gentle, not quarrelsome, not a lover of money. He must manage his own family well and see that his children obey him with proper respect" (1 Timothy 3:1–4).

In other words, let your kids see you live your life as you instruct them to live, and try to live "above reproach." For example, many times we hear of the "cycle of violence." How many abused young boys grow up to abuse others? It doesn't take a nuclear physicist to figure out that our children are clay, and we mold them by our actions as well as our words. They are sponges, and they will soak up clean, pure water and they will soak up stains. We cannot directly determine every influence in their lives, especially as they get older. But, we can start early, and provide as much pure, clear, and clean water as we can to our little sponges; nothing is purer and cleaner than God's word. The fruit of the spirit is a perfect starting place for our children, even if they are too young to understand completely God's message of forgiveness and salvation.

Sharing Your Faith

Finally, the public at large considers many Christians, and particularly evangelical or fundamentalist Christians, as self-righteous know-it-alls. Much of this view is fashioned and promoted by our left-leaning mainstream media, but much of it is also the product of the well-documented duplicity of Jim and Tammy Faye Bakker, Jimmy Swaggart, and others. Thus, when telling others of the love of Christ, and sharing God's good news of forgiveness and salvation, we must proceed gently and with respect for those we seek to influence. Don't hide your love of Christ, and the joy that your personal relationship with Jesus holds for you, but tread lightly when holding yourself up as an example of one who leads a Christian life. "But in your hearts set apart Christ as Lord. Always be prepared to give an answer to everyone who asks you to give the reason for the hope that you have. But do this with gentleness and respect, keeping a clear conscience, so that those who speak maliciously against your good behavior in Christ may be ashamed of their slander" (1 Peter 3:15, 16).

No one is without sin. As I mentioned previously, writing this book is as convicting for me as it may be for those who read it. There are many things I need to work on daily as well. We all face different temptations, troubles, and strife, and we all have different external influences with which to deal—our bosses, spouses, children, financial pressures, worldly temptations, etc.

Many times it is difficult for us to share the gospel with others because of our own shortcomings and failures. In fact, Peter asks us to give reasons for our faith with a clear conscience to those who ask you about the "hope that you have," but also with respect and gentleness. Although God's message is just and pure, we are not without blame and without sin. By acknowledging that we are not perfect, and that accepting Christ doesn't mean that we no longer make mistakes, we humble ourselves (but not God) before those who desperately need to hear his message. We can steer clear of the attack of hypocrisy by admitting that we are not perfect and that we are works in progress, and telling others that the good news of the gospel is that a price has already been paid for our failures and our sins, and that sincere repentance results in true forgiveness.

On the other hand, we obviously cannot ignore God's word and continue living in the darkness rather than the light, and expect to 1) influence others around us positively to accept Christ and apply the fruit of the spirit to their lives, and 2) continue earning God's faithful forgiveness of our sins. As so clearly stated in 1 John, God expects that we will sin, and He will faithfully forgive us if we humbly and sincerely repent and strive to turn from sin. However, continued or repeated sinning scoffs at God's gift of forgiveness. Trust me, God knows your heart.

In sum, when sharing your faith to others, whether openly or whether you've been asked, do so in a way that is natural for you. Are you quiet and unassuming? Do you share by simply shining as a light to God through your good deeds, kindness, and caring of others? Or, are you more vocal and open? Do you share by participating in "kindness explosions" or free car washes in the name of Christ? Do you have special talents, such as writing or playing a musical instrument, or do you have a wonderful voice? Do you share by writing letters to the editor, or writing poems, books, or church bulletin articles? Do you share by singing God's praises in the choir or in public? Do you share by playing an instrument in the praise band at church, or in a public park? Or, do you share one on one, recommending Christian books like this one to your co-workers or friends, or inviting them to your church or Bible study, but in a subtle but kind way? All such outreach should be done with kindness, gentleness, and respect, just as Jesus reached out to us, in a manner of sacrifice, giving, healing, kindness, gentleness, and love.

Chapter IX.

Self-Control

Be self-controlled and alert. Your enemy the devil prowls around like a roaring lion looking for someone to devour. Resist him, standing firm in the faith, because you know that your brothers throughout the world are undergoing the same kind of sufferings. (1 Peter 5:8, 9)

Self-control is not considered a virtue, especially in modern-day America. What is our cultural threshold or tolerance for the level of filth we will permit into our lives and into homes via TV or movies? Is it the same standard Paul, Peter, or even Christ would use? What is our tolerance for sexual immorality among our leaders or for ourselves? Bill Clinton obviously attempted to redefine the phrase "sexual relations" in describing his lewd acts in the White House with an intern. Our former Commander- in-Chief exhibited no self-control; no faithfulness to his spouse, his family, or his country; and no commitment to love. What kind of message does this send to our youth in America? That same former President then committed perjury in an attempt to justify his sleazy affair. Clinton's actions simply reinforce what we are taught in America through our "me" centric culture—"go for it"; "just do it"; "you deserve it." Why shouldn't a millionaire indulge himself with five or six luxury cars? Why shouldn't a movie or rock star engage in as many one-night stands as he or she has concerts? Why shouldn't we smoke another pack of cigarettes, or eat a second bowl of ice cream? Why shouldn't the most powerful political leader in the world have his way with an intern?

As discussed previously, God has given us a world filled with great abundance, which we are encouraged to enjoy. I don't believe God is drawing a line in the sand at your third slice of a good pizza. The line between moderation and gluttony is a difficult one to define. I do not have all of the answers, but God does. If we pray sincerely to Him for guidance, I believe He will help us shun selfish desires and sinful temptations. The scriptures also teach us that temperance and moderation are the keys to enjoying God's great earthly gifts, and not bowing down to them as gods of our lives. Consider 2 Peter 1:3–7, in which Peter speaks of God's great gift of eternal life and his plea for us to make every effort at self-control: "His divine power *has given us everything we need for life* and godliness through our knowledge of him who called us by his own glory and goodness. Through these he has given us *his very great and precious promises*, so that through them you may participate in the divine nature and escape the corruption in the world caused by evil desires. For this very reason, make every effort to add to your faith goodness; and to goodness, knowledge; and to knowledge, *self-control*; and to self-control, perseverance; and to perseverance, godliness; and to godliness, brotherly kindness; and to brotherly kindness, love" (italics added).

As Peter also claims in 1 Peter 5, Satan is prowling around us with countless temptations, attempting to use God's great gifts to us as weapons against us and our families. Again, we all succumb to different temptations, and Satan knows which buttons to push. For some, it is food; for others, sex, power, or status; and still others, shoes, cars, jewelry, gambling boats, or sports books. Reflect back to the other chapters. Consider the extent to which self-control, or the lack thereof, destroys the fruit of the spirit in our lives. It literally wilts and spoils the fruit we are to nurture, water, and feed in our lives. For example:

> *Our true love is corrupted by adultery or lust after someone or something.*
>
> It is God's will that you should be sanctified: that you should avoid sexual immorality; that each of you should learn to control his own body in a way that is holy and honorable, not in passionate lust like the heathen, who do not know God. (1 Thessalonians 4:3–5)

> *Our joy is stolen from us when we obsess over our material possessions—consumerism.*
>
> Whoever loves money never has money enough; whoever loves wealth is never satisfied with his income. This too is meaningless. (Ecclesiastes 5:10)

> *Our peace is shattered by the consequences of our addiction to—and obsession with—food, drugs, alcohol or gambling.*
>
> It is not good to eat too much honey, nor is it honorable to seek one's own honor. Like a city whose walls are broken down is a man who lacks self-control. (Proverbs 25:27, 28)

> *Our patience is ruined by our inability to control our emotions when faced with a bawling child.*
>
> A fool gives full vent to his anger, but a wise man keeps himself under control. (Proverbs 29:11)

Our kindness and goodness toward others is overrun by our selfishness.

Do nothing out of selfish ambition or vain conceit, but in humility consider others better than yourselves. Each of you should look not only to your own interests, but also to the interests of others. (Philippians 2:3, 4)

Our faithfulness to God and to our families is swept under the rug by long hours at work, and our inability to control our obsession with the next promotion, the next pat on the back, or the next bonus.

No servant can serve two masters. Either he will hate the one and love the other, or he will be devoted to the one and despise the other. You cannot serve both God and Money. (Luke 16:13)

Our gentleness converts into verbal or physical abuse if we can't control our temper or we allow drugs to drive the Holy Spirit from our hearts.

Those who live according to the sinful nature have their minds set on what that nature desires; but those who live in accordance with the Spirit have their minds set on what the Spirit desires. The mind of sinful man is death, but the mind controlled by the Spirit is life and peace. (Romans 8:5, 6)

Submit your mind to the Holy Spirit, not to your sinful nature, and resist Satan's pull. We are warned throughout the Bible of Satan's attempts to wrest control of Christians from the safe haven of the Holy Spirit, but once we submit to God fully, Satan will recoil: "Submit yourselves, then, to God. Resist the devil, and he will flee from you" (James 4:7). But again, we must remain alert and self-controlled as our "enemy the devil prowls around like a roaring lion looking for someone to devour." Satan will look for opportunities where you let your guard down, unknowingly allowing him to slither back into your life. Obviously, self-control is not only a vital component to unlocking the fruit of the spirit within each of us, but the lack of self-control can itself lead to our downfall, whether or not we are Christians.

Note that many times when the word "self-control" is mentioned in the Bible, including in Galatians 5:22, it is joined together with words like "love," "faith," "pure," "Godliness," and "goodness." For example, consider Second Titus:

> Teach the older men to be temperate, worthy of respect, *self-controlled*, and sound in faith, in love and in endurance. Likewise, teach the older women to be reverent in the way they live, not to be slanderers or addicted to much wine, but to teach what is good. Then they can train the younger women to love their husbands and children, to be *self-controlled* and pure, to be busy at home, to be kind, and to be subject to their husbands, so that no one will malign the word of God. Similarly, encourage the young men to be *self-controlled*. (Titus 2:2–6, italics added)

> For the grace of God that brings salvation has appeared to all men. It teaches us to say "No" to ungodliness and worldly passions, and to live *self-controlled*, upright and godly lives in this present age, while we wait for the blessed hope—the glorious appearing of our great God and Savior, Jesus Christ, who gave himself for us to redeem us from all wickedness and to purify for himself a people that are his very own, eager to do what is good. (Titus 2:11–14, italics added)

Thus, self-control really embodies every one of the other

fruit of the spirit. In other words, if we are truly to apply the fruit of the spirit to our daily lives, and grow in Christ's love, we must pray for, and practice, self-control. As Jesus commanded, pray the Lord's Prayer, which includes the words "lead us not into temptation, but deliver us from the evil one" (Matthew 6:13). God "will not let you be tempted beyond what you can bear. But when you are tempted, he will also provide a way out so that you can stand up under it" (1 Corinthians 10:13). God understands that self-control is difficult for us in the face of immense earthly temptations, especially given our own weak minds, and He has given us a way out through Him. If we do not humble ourselves before God and pray for his guiding hand, our relationships, our minds, and even our faith hang by a thread—in great jeopardy.

Conclusion

He then brought them out and asked, "Sirs, what must I do to be saved?" They replied, "Believe in the Lord Jesus, and you will be saved—you and your household." (Acts 16:30, 31)

As you may have surmised by now, the first step to reaping a bountiful harvest of the fruit of the spirit in your life, and hopefully in the lives of those you love, is to believe in Jesus Christ and to trust Him with your entire life and being. Once you have made this affirmative step, and humbled yourself before the Lord, you will receive the magnificent gift of eternal life. "For it is by grace you have been saved, through faith—and this not from yourselves, it is the gift of God" (Ephesians 2:8). Do not fight the urge to turn your life over to Him if you haven't done so, or if you feel the call to recommit yourself to Him. Recall the words of doubting Thomas in John 14:5–7: "Thomas said to him, 'Lord, we don't know where you are going, so how can we know the way?' Jesus answered, 'I am the way and the truth and the life. No one comes to the Father except through me. If you really knew me, you would know my Father as well.

From now on, you do know him and have seen him.'" Jesus claims clearly that the *only* way to the Father is through His Son. Jesus is the way (the path to the Father), the truth (the fulfillment of Old Testament prophesies—the only man to never have sinned and the one teacher who spoke in God's absolute truths), and the life (the eternal life that God grants us if we submit our lives to His Son).

Consider also the well-known passage John 3:16, 17: "For God so loved the world that he gave his one and only Son, that whoever believes in him shall not perish but have eternal life. For God did not send his Son into the world to condemn the world, but to save the world through him." God made the ultimate sacrifice of His Son out of His tremendous love for us, although none of us deserved such grace. He "loved" the world so much that He provided a simple, yet majestic, path to Him through the blood of Christ. Without God's gift, "the wages of sin is death" (Romans 6:23). Jesus paid for our sins, and those of the entire world, so that we can freely accept God's gift of eternal life.

If we accept, what then happens? How are we to live? We are essentially reborn as children of God. Unfortunately, our mainstream media uses the term "born again Christian" in a a derogatory manner, along with "right wing" or "conservative" Christians. However, the Bible does not so distinguish between types of Christians. Bear in mind Jesus' words in John 3:3–7: "I tell you the truth, *no one can see the kingdom of God unless he is born again.*" "How can a man be born when he is old?" Nicodemus asked. "Surely he cannot enter a second time into his mother's womb to be born!" Jesus answered, "I tell you the truth, no one can enter the kingdom of God unless he is born of water and the Spirit. Flesh gives birth to flesh, but the Spirit gives birth to spirit. You should not be surprised at my saying, '*You must be born again*'" (italics added).

Yes, for those shaking their heads in disbelief, Jesus

spoke these words not once, but twice, as recorded in the Gospel of John. True Christians are *all* born again. Jesus' point here is that God's gift of eternal life comes through a personal relationship with Him, which results in a rebirth of each believer as a new child of God with Jesus at the core of his or her heart. Once we've accepted Christ, God's kingdom dwells within our hearts and will be unleashed upon Christ's return. "Just as man is destined to die once, and after that to face judgment, so Christ was sacrificed once to take away the sins of many people; and he will appear a second time, not to bear sin, but to bring salvation to those who are waiting for him" (Hebrews 9:27, 28).

Now that God's path to salvation is so crystal clear, what must we affirmatively do to attain eternal life and to enter God's kingdom? There is no formal way of turning oneself over to Christ, but most Christians have recited some version of the "sinner's prayer," in which one commits his or her life to Christ, repents of past sins, thanks Jesus for His sacrifice, acknowledges His glorious resurrection, and pledges to live life as a new creation. "If anyone is in Christ, he is a new creation; the old has gone, the new has come!" (2 Corinthians 5:17). "To all who received him, to those who believed in his name, he gave the right to become children of God—children born not of natural descent, nor of human decision or a husband's will, but born of God" (John 1:12, 13). Such rebirth should change our attitudes, desires, emotions, and actions. Such rebirth should also cause us to carefully study and examine the word of God, and practice the fruit of the spirit daily.

We all want God's peace, His forgiveness, and His love, and if you've read this book, by now you fully understand God's message and his path to receiving His gift of eternal life and understand His call for us to love one another. Paul simply sums up the path to eternal life, which is available to all who confess and believe, in Romans 10:9–13: "That if you confess with your mouth, 'Jesus is Lord,' and believe in your heart that God raised him from the dead, you will be saved. For it is with your heart that you believe and are justified, and it is with your mouth that you confess and are saved. As the Scripture says, 'Anyone who trusts in him will never be put to shame.' For there is no difference between Jew and Gentile—the same Lord is Lord of all and richly blesses all who call on him, for, *'Everyone who calls on the name of the Lord will be saved'* " (italics added).

Anyone can be saved. *Everyone* can be saved. God is faithful and patient. I didn't accept Christ as my savior until I was twenty-five years old. Like many Americans, I believed in God and that Jesus was His Son. I celebrated Christian holidays, albeit mostly only recognizing the "Americanized" versions of such holidays, with little mention of Jesus' birth or resurrection, and instead dominated by visions of Santa, the Easter Bunny and shopping. I had never read the Bible, rarely attended church, and had never turned my life over to Christ. I just didn't get the concept. I scorned most Christians essentially due to my own feelings of inadequacy: "I'm not good enough for God," and "I don't know the scripture well enough to go to church." If you too feel that way or have felt that way, church homes are out there that will take you with open arms. The message of salvation is to be preached to the ends of the earth, and God knows, and Christians know, that everyone comes to Jesus in his own time. Whether nine or seventy-nine, it is never too late to come to Christ. He is faithful, and He is waiting to defend you on your day of judgment. If you're still struggling with the concept, consider the following anonymous email that has been circulating among Christians on the internet for some time:

> After living a "decent" life, my time on earth came
> to an end. The first thing I remember is sitting on a
> bench in the waiting room of what I thought to be a

courthouse. The doors opened and I was instructed to come in and have a seat by the defense table. As I looked around I saw the "prosecutor." He was a villainous-looking gent who snarled as he stared at me. He definitely was the most evil person I have ever seen. I sat down and looked to my left and there sat my lawyer, a kind and gentle-looking man whose appearance seemed familiar to me.

The corner door flew open and there appeared the judge in full flowing robes. He commanded an awesome presence as he moved across the room. I couldn't take my eyes off of him. As he took his seat behind the bench, he said, "Let us begin." The prosecutor rose and said, "My name is Satan, and I am here to show you why this man belongs in hell." He proceeded to tell of lies that I told, things that I stole, and in the past when I cheated others. Satan told of other horrible perversions that were once in my life, and the more he spoke, the further down in my seat I sank. I was so embarrassed that I couldn't look at anyone, even my own lawyer, as the Devil told of sins that even I had completely forgotten about.

As upset as I was at Satan for telling all these things about me, I was equally upset at my representative who sat there silently, not offering any form of defense at all. I know I had been guilty of those things, but I had done some good in my life—couldn't that at least equal out part of the harm I'd done? Satan finished with a fury and said, "This man belongs in hell—he is guilty of all that I have charged, and there is not a person who can prove otherwise.

When it was his turn, my lawyer first asked if he might approach the bench. The judge allowed this over the strong objection of Satan, and beckoned him to come forward. As he got up and started walking, I was able to see him in his full splendor and majesty. I realized why he seemed so familiar. This was Jesus representing me—my Lord and my Savior. He stopped at the bench and softly said to the judge, "Hi Dad," and then he turned to address the court. "Satan was correct in saying that this man had sinned, I won't deny any of these allegations. And yes, the wage of sin is death, and this man deserves to be punished." Jesus took a deep breath and turned to his Father with outstretched arms and proclaimed, "However, I died on the cross so that this person might have eternal life, and he has accepted me as his Savior, so he is mine." My Lord continued with, "His name is written in the book of life and no one can snatch him from me. Satan still does not understand yet. This man is not to be given justice, but rather mercy." As Jesus sat down, he quietly paused, looked at his Father and replied, "There is nothing else that needs to be done. I've done it all."

The judge lifted his mighty hand and slammed the gavel down. The following words bellowed from his lips: "This man is free, the penalty for him has already been paid in full; case dismissed." As my Lord led me away, I could hear Satan ranting and raving, "I won't give up! I'll win the next one!" I asked Jesus as he gave me my instructions where to go next, "Have you ever lost a case?" Christ lovingly smiled and said, "Everyone that has come to me and asked me to represent him has received the same verdict as you: Paid in Full."

Once saved, you can begin living a life of love, joy, peace, patience, kindness, goodness, faithfulness, gentleness, and self-control, and can be free from the "constraints" on your "freedom" that you once associated with Christianity. Harvesting the fruit of the spirit in all of your relationships, whether with God, your loved ones, or even strangers, will bring you closer to your full potential as one of God's children.

In conclusion, in this short book I do not profess to address every manner in which the fruit of the spirit may be cultivated in your own life. However, hopefully it will encourage you to explore God's word more deeply and to harvest the fruit of the spirit in your own life in your own unique circumstances. Good luck and may God bless you, your relationships, and your family as you either begin a new journey with Christ, or you continue on a journey begun long ago!